Praise for

A Good and Perfect
Faith, Expectations, and a Little

Becker . . . knows how to grab a reader's heartstrings and never let go as she writes about her journey as a new mom to Penny, her first child, who has Down syndrome. This beautifully written text explores how Becker and her husband deal with the news of having a child with a disability and the transformation they undergo as time passes. Becker's work is introspective and theologically inquisitive, leading readers to ask the same questions this mother asks herself as her world tilted off its axis.

—*Publishers Weekly*
starred review

Amy Julia Becker makes herself vulnerable to enlighten us, not just about Down syndrome, but about the intrinsic gifts of life. This book is a must-read, and not just for families and friends of children with Down syndrome.

—Sara Groves
singer and songwriter

Amy Julia Becker has the courage and grace to tell the truth. Whether you are a parent or not, whether the children in your life are "typical" or not, her story will shake you, change you, and encourage you. In a world obsessed with achievement and perfection, *A Good and Perfect Gift* opens the door to a much more excellent way.

—Andy Crouch
author, *Culture Making*

This excellent and moving book about Penny as a wonderful gift should be read not just by parents of people with disabilities but by all of us who should discover the beauty of those who are different.

—Jean Vanier
author, founder L'Arche

It has been said there are places in our hearts we do not even know until the heart is broken. *A Good and Perfect Gift* is the moving story of how Amy Julia Becker and her husband found their hearts broken through the arrival of their very special child. There is beauty here—in the writing and the story—told with deep feeling and faith but not sentimentality. I recommend this book highly, not only to parents with a special child, but to all who seek to discern what God gives us through some of our most painful times.

—Leighton Ford
author, *The Attentive Life*

Do not be fooled. This is not a typical book about disabilities, sorrow, and triumph. This is a book about a mother who loves her daughter: "I needed to see her as our little girl, not as a diagnosis, not as an obstacle to overcome." This is among the best books I have read about the true power of the powerless.

—Christopher de Vinck
author, *The Power of the Powerless*

It takes faith to turn an unmet expectation into something delightfully exceptional, and Amy Julia Becker learned to do just that when Penny was born. Poignant and powerful, the world needs more stories of inspiration like this one!

—Joni Eareckson Tada
Joni and Friends International Disability Center

A forthright account of a how a mother used her religious faith to come to terms of adjustment, acceptance, and love for having a child with Down syndrome.

—Dr. Carl Pickhardt
psychologist, author, child development expert

Amy Julia's rare gift with words—descriptive, vulnerable, penetrating—bring to life a message of joyful contentment inspired by her daughter Penny.

—Susan Alexander Yates
author and speaker

a good and perfect gift

Faith, Expectations, and a Little Girl Named Penny

AMY JULIA BECKER

BETHANY HOUSE PUBLISHERS
a division of Baker Publishing Group
Minneapolis, Minnesota

Published by Bethany House Publishers
11400 Hampshire Avenue South
Bloomington, Minnesota 55438
www.bethanyhouse.com

Bethany House Publishers is a division of
Baker Publishing Group, Grand Rapids, Michigan

Printed in the United States of America

Library of Congress Cataloging-in-Publication Data

Becker, Amy Julia.
A good and perfect gift : faith, expectations, and a little girl named Penny / Amy Julia Becker.
p. cm.
Summary: "A memoir of a young mom finding joy in her daughter with Down Syndrome, as she learns that unmet expectations can bring peace and freedom"—Provided by publisher.
ISBN 978-0-7642-0917-8 (pbk. : alk. paper)
1. Becker, Penelope Truesdell, 2005– 2. Becker, Amy Julia—Family. 3. Down syndrome—Patients—Biography. 4. Children with mental disabilities—United States—Biography. 5. Parents of children with disabilities—Biography. I. Title.
RJ506.D68B434 2011
618.92′8588420092—dc23 2011025204

Cover design by Greg Jackson, Thinkpen Design, Inc.
Cover photograph by Maria Jose Rivera/Trevillion Images

Author is represented by Foundry Literary & Media

11 12 13 14 15 16 17 7 6 5 4 3 2 1

In keeping with biblical principles of creation stewardship, Baker Publishing Group advocates the responsible use of our natural resources. As a member of the Green Press Initiative, our company uses recycled paper when possible. The text paper of this book is composed in part of post-consumer waste.

Hope is the thing with feathers
That perches in the soul,
And sings the song without the words,
And never stops at all.
—Emily Dickinson

Every good and perfect gift is from above . . .
James 1:17

contents

author's note

The events in this book are true to life, although some details have been compressed. The names of individuals have been changed, with the exception of my immediate family and the Fords. Virginia is based primarily upon one brave friend. One day we were talking about this book, and she said, "I think you need to include the stupid things that people say. And I know I've said a lot of them, so I'll volunteer myself for the job." Some comments that Virginia makes, however, came from the lips of others, so her character has become a compilation of friends. Also, as I hope the story itself demonstrates, the "stupid" comments always occurred in the context of compassion and love, for which I am quite grateful.

Many thanks, therefore, to "Virginia" and to Mom and Dad, Kate, Brooks, and Elly, for your willingness to allow me to share parts of who you are. Thanks also for the support of friends from The Lawrenceville School, Westerly Road Church, and the Down Syndrome Association of Central New Jersey. Thanks to Matt Novenson, David Dicosimo, and Kevin Hector for offering your expertise on theological matters. Areta, once again I thank you for putting me through creative writing graduate school without needing to pay tuition.

To my agent, Chris Park, thanks for hanging in there with me and for your devotion to this project. To my editor, Andy McGuire, and the rest of the team at Bethany—I can't thank you enough for taking a risk with this book and for all your hard work and encouragement along the way. Thanks to Peter, for your tireless support as I wrote these words—both in journal form many years ago and in manuscript form more recently. And even greater thanks for your willingness to walk this road with me every step of the way.

I'm also grateful for all the other families out there with children with disabilities. Whether because of social stigma or as a result of physical suffering, countless parents and children have endured far greater hardship than we have. Your perseverance and love pioneered a way for us. Thank you.

Finally, thank you, Penny, for opening our eyes to a world of beauty, delight, and hope.

prologue

If only we had waited. If only I were due in the summer. Then I could have finished school. Then Peter would have three months free from teaching. Having this baby in June instead of January, that would make sense.

I jerked the car out of the parking lot and rested one hand on top of my round belly. As I drove past a little white church and a deli and a graveyard, I had a thought—and it was so powerful it was more like hearing than thinking—*But if you had waited, then you wouldn't have had* this *child.*

And all my objections ceased.

You wouldn't have had this *child. . . .*

PART ONE

this child

I love the intimacy of feeling her kick and wriggle and push inside me. I love lying on my side pressed up against Peter and hearing him laugh whenever she moves and he can feel it on his thigh. I love that we are already loving her together.

From my journal, October 2005

1

"You didn't like dolls," my mother said. "You would put all your puzzles in a row in the playroom and dump their pieces onto the floor, then put them back together one by one."

She shook her head as she unloaded the dishwasher. Then she turned toward me with a smile. "The only word you said incorrectly was *raisins*. Those, for some reason, you called 'sha sha.' Otherwise, you wouldn't speak unless you could say the word properly."

I smiled, a little amused, a little self-conscious. Mom wiped her hands on a dish towel. Her curly brown hair was pulled back with two barrettes. Dressed in a Santa Claus sweater and snowflake earrings, she looked her part—preschool teacher, mother of four, grandmother-to-be.

It was the day after Christmas. I was helping put away the china and silver from dinner the night before, but I soon leaned against the hutch in her kitchen, my hand pressed against my lower back. My belly was a taut globe, an announcement to the world that our child would arrive any day now. Our child. Our daughter. Penny.

Mom stacked the plates and placed them on open shelves filled with holiday cheer in the form of elves, snowflakes, miniature sleighs, and jingle bells. She closed the top of the box that held the silver and tucked it under the counter. "I have a few different options for lunch," she said.

She poured chili into one pot and carrot-ginger soup into another as I stacked red bowls on the counter and retrieved the everyday silverware. "Anything else?"

She motioned toward the chairs. "I've got the rest. You sit down."

It all felt comfortable, familiar—the paper whites blooming in the window, the smell of another home-cooked meal, the kitchen drawer that needed repair, the skylights, the sight of Mom at work.

The house was filled with reminders of my childhood. The window ledge spanning the length of the dining room held a line of family photos—one from every Christmas since my birth. I could walk through my life, starting as an only child gazing with wonder at a tree full of lights. Then, with my baby sister Kate, wearing a "falalalala" dress that Mom had made of red corduroy with white letters. On down the line, with Brooks and Elly entering the family, and from there through the ruffles and taffeta of middle school to the long blond hair of high school to the black pants and sweater that had become my uniform as a young working woman. Still, through it all, I resembled the little girl Mom had described—the one who liked books more than toys, the one who always acted a little more grown-up than her age.

That evening we all gathered in the attic, a makeshift family room that remained unpainted and without heat, home to old dress-up clothes, rows of *National Geographic* magazines, an L-shaped couch, and a big-screen TV. Brooks and Elly shared a blanket. Kate curled up in a chair with a cup of hot chocolate. Mom and Dad sat side by side, their bodies not quite touching. I leaned against Peter, his hand resting on me, waiting for the sharp kicks and ripples that always came in the evening. It still seemed mysterious—that my body could join with his and form another person. That she would inherit my round cheeks or his dark hair or my grandfather's chin. That she would be ours, and yet utterly herself all at the same time.

Brooks and Elly had decided we should watch some old home videos, but as they flipped through the choices, my mind lingered on the more immediate past, the preparations for new life among us. I had read a host of baby books and written thank-you notes for the dozens of presents we had already accumulated. We had attended a day-long session at the hospital for expectant parents. I learned techniques to breathe through pain, and a nurse walked us through the birthing process. We peeked inside one of the delivery rooms. I had already written all my final papers for graduate school, just in case she came early. And yet, despite the preparations, despite my body's insistence that a baby was coming, I couldn't believe we were going to be parents, I was going to be a mother. I squeezed Peter's hand when she kicked again.

Brooks and Elly agreed on a series of classics—first Brooks as a three-year-old making up a song for the camera: "Why do I have to live in this canoe?" Then Elly as a four-year-old newscaster reporting on the weather. Then the four of us, that same year, when I was thirteen, producing a video for Mom and Dad's twentieth wedding anniversary as we mimicked their daily routines. And then, there I was, two years old with bleach-blond hair and big green eyes, singing a college fight song. In the video it was summertime, and my mother was pregnant with Kate. Someone asked me when the new baby was coming. "In Octoder," I replied, and then corrected myself with a frown and a shake of the head. "In October."

Even at age two I had to get it exactly right. It had to be perfect.

Back at our own apartment a few nights later, I woke up with a stomachache. After two hours curled in a chair reading, I padded down the long hallway from the living room to our bedroom, shaking my head. I had seen my doctor the day before, and I could still hear her words: "You aren't dilated at all. You haven't dropped. It will be another week or two at least."

I reached the bedroom and nudged Peter's shoulder. "I might be having contractions."

He rolled toward me and squinted into the light. "Really?"

"It's probably false labor," I said, trying to sound calm. I glanced at the clock. Six a.m. "But I want to get the nursery ready. Just in case."

He looked as if he were holding back a smile as he pushed himself up.

I shrugged, a little embarrassed that all I could think about were the tasks I wanted to accomplish. But then my torso tightened. I clenched my teeth and breathed through my nose. *False labor,* I told myself again. With the contraction over, I forced a smile. "Ready?"

Peter was a teacher and a housemaster in a boarding school, so we lived in an apartment within a dormitory of thirty high school boys, a century-old building of burgundy brick with copper gutters and a slate roof. The back of the apartment held two bedrooms that once had been the quarters for a cook and a maid. They were odd configurations with slanted walls and uneven ceilings. Penny's room backed up to ours. It held a double bed, a crib, a chair, and a changing table, but the walls were bare.

That morning I washed all the baby clothes. We hung pictures, mostly keepsakes from our own childhoods. The embroidered alphabet my mother made me as an infant. Peter's christening announcement. A painting of a teddy bear. Peter bounded from pushing the crib into the corner of the room to hammering another nail into the wall, as though he were playing an intense and thoroughly enjoyable tennis match. I moved more slowly, without his giddy energy. If I allowed myself to feel excited, then I would have to think about what lay ahead, the unknown intensity of labor and delivery. Excitement would soon give way to fear, so I kept my thoughts focused on arranging pictures and starting another load of laundry until, every twenty minutes or so, the pain would arrive, and I'd clutch Peter's hand or press my palms against the cool plaster of the yellow wall and say to myself, as if it were a mantra, *False labor. False labor.*

It took about three hours to get the clothes washed and folded and to fill the walls of Penny's room. "I guess I should call the doctor," I said, once there was nothing left to do.

Another hour and three contractions later, we arrived at the hospital. Peter had showered and shaved, and I had pulled my hair back into a ponytail and put on a little makeup. Dr. Mayer examined me and said, "I can feel your baby's head. You're here to stay."

I wanted to laugh and cry all at once. My eyes met Peter's. He leaned over and kissed my belly, then gave me a lingering kiss on the lips. "I'll run home and pack our bags."

"And would you call my mom?" I asked as he headed for the door.

I found myself attended to by two nurses at once, my clothes in a heap and a hospital gown over my head and a strap around my middle to monitor the strength of the contractions along with Penny's heart rate. A prick in the vein on top of my hand and an IV dripping fluid into my bloodstream.

And then, just as abruptly, they were gone. I noticed my surroundings for the first time—a small, windowless rectangle with bare white walls. I vaguely remembered a nurse saying, "We'll get you your own room as soon as possible," and I realized another patient lay on the other side of a curtain. She spoke only Spanish, but as nurses came and went, I understood that she was in labor at twenty weeks gestation. She was carrying twins.

Every time a nurse came to her side, I wanted to call out, but the words wouldn't come. My situation—the rather mundane pain of labor—couldn't compare to the fear she must have been feeling for the lives of those babies. I lay still, and my contractions marched forward until they arrived every five minutes. I watched the screen that measured their intensity and felt an odd sense of awe as the line shot to the top of the graph and held steady for sixty solid seconds. Pain smothered me. It took me an hour to muster the courage to say, "Excuse me? I'd like an epidural. Please."

It wasn't much longer until Peter returned. I caught a glimpse of him before we made eye contact, and I felt my shoulders relax knowing he was nearby. *After six years of marriage, he still makes me feel like a teenager*, I thought, as I took in his strong jawline and wavy black hair and broad shoulders. And now, even though I knew there was more pain to come, his presence steadied me.

They moved me into a private room—big and bright, with picture windows spanning the horizon. An anesthesiologist arrived to start the epidural, and soon it had numbed my body from the waist down. Now all I had to do was wait. Peter went about setting up speakers so we could listen to music. My mother and sisters arrived. They walked in quietly, but I could see the excitement on their faces. Kate's eyes sparkled. Elly looked as if she might laugh. Brooks clapped her hands together when she saw me, but then she stopped herself as if she needed permission to continue.

"Hello, everybody," I said, setting aside the most recent issue of *The New Yorker*. "No need to tiptoe. The epidural is working its magic. I can't feel a thing."

Kate let out a little cry. "I can't believe this is really happening!"

Mom gave me a quick kiss on the forehead and turned to greet Peter.

Brooks shimmied her shoulders, as if she might start dancing. The three of them crowded around the bed.

I said, "I'm so glad you can all be here."

"I'm glad you're early," Elly replied. "I would've been back at school if you'd waited until your due date."

I was seventeen days early—not enough to be considered premature, but enough to surprise us all.

"Okay," Brooks said. "Wait a minute. I still don't understand. How are you so calm right now?"

I pointed to the screen. "It's all about the epidural. When that line shoots to the top, it means I'm having another contraction. I just can't feel them anymore."

"I'd say you've been pretty calm all day," Peter said.

I told the family the story so far. Then they reviewed their afternoon—Peter's phone call, driving around town to find Mom on a walk with a friend, throwing clothes in bags and piling into the car.

"Dad's going to come tomorrow," Mom said.

I nodded, thinking that Dad wouldn't know what to do with himself through the hours of waiting. But Mom and my sisters seemed happy to be here now. The energy in the room was palpable, like the giddy anticipation of kids on Christmas morning.

We didn't have to wait long. About an hour after my family arrived, Dr. Mayer checked in again. "It's time to push," she said. "We're a little short-staffed, since this is a holiday weekend." She turned to my mother. "Mom, think you can help?"

Mom certainly had experience—four deliveries of her own, and one of those without a doctor present. He had walked in with my father, who had been away on a business trip, five minutes after Elly was born. Now Mom pushed up the sleeves of her white turtleneck and took her position holding my left leg. Peter, on the right, was my coach. He never stopped looking at me, and his voice held a mixture of gravitas and pride as he said again and again, "You can do this. Push."

But I couldn't figure it out. I couldn't feel anything. I was doing something wrong. I was failing. Failing. A monitor started to beep.

"The baby's heart rate is dropping," Dr. Mayer said. She turned to a nurse. "Page the neonatologist." And then she looked at me, equally stern. "When the next contraction comes, you have to push. You have got to get this baby out."

Somehow, my body knew what to do. With the next contraction, Dr. Mayer cheered. "You're on your way. Okay. Okay."

Two pushes later, Penny shot into the world. I caught a glimpse of her wriggling body and heard squawks from her little lungs. With a weary, delighted smile, I lay back. Peter held both sides of my face and choked out the words, "You did it. We did it. She's beautiful." He kissed me and held my hand tight.

"Eight out of ten on her Apgar," someone said.

I turned my head, following my daughter. The neonatologist had just arrived. Her presence seemed unnecessary now. She examined Penny and washed her off, wrapped her in a blanket, and placed her in my arms. Penny had a full head of black hair and pouty lips, and she opened her eyes just long enough for me to see that they were deep blue, the color of a lake on a cloudy day. And then she was gone.

It was all action and congratulations from there—Peter announcing the good news, my body starting to respond to the intensity of what it had just experienced, shaking, teeth chattering, my sisters exclaiming how cute Penny looked when they saw her through the glass walls of the nursery. We called my dad, his dad, his brother, a whole list of friends. Peter even called his boss so he could send an email to the rest of the faculty: Penelope Truesdell Becker, five pounds, five ounces, nineteen inches, born at 5:22 p.m. on December 30, 2005. Alleluia and Happy New Year!

Amidst the euphoria, amidst the doctor's report that Penny was a little cold and they would bring her in when she had warmed up, a nurse called Peter out of the room. In the back of my brain, a warning signal flashed. I was in the middle of giving directions for Mom and my sisters to get some dinner and was more attuned to my own body than anything else—this mushy midsection that hours before held a baby, these shaky limbs, the ache that began to creep into my back. My legs tingled. Adrenaline seeped out of my bloodstream, leaving me dazed, content.

When Peter returned, my eyes were drawn to a speck of blood on the collar of his red-and-white checked shirt. It took me a minute to realize the blood was mine. Only then did I notice that his eyes were brimming. He grasped my hand. "The doctors think Penny has Down syndrome."

I kept staring at that speck of blood, trying to differentiate it from the red of the shirt, wondering whether it would come out in the wash or whether it would be a permanent reminder of Penny's birth. That speck of blood.

Peter said, "Age?" using his nickname for me.

I shook my head. The only word that came to mind was *No*.

The lines in his face were soft and his tone was gentle, careful. "She has some of the features of a Down's baby, I guess. The doctors said they can come talk to you if you have any questions."

"Okay," I said with a nod.

The world began to break into pieces, as if I had been looking at a scene through a plate-glass window that suddenly cracked, jagged lines distorting my vision. I had a flash of anger—*How dare they talk to Peter without me?* And then a flash of concern—*Is Penny okay?* And soon they were standing there, the neonatologist, a woman with thin brown hair who never smiled, and the pediatrician, a round-faced man with sweaty palms. I thought, *They don't know what to say.* My voice clenched, but I didn't cry. I argued with them a little, as if I could convince them to take back their pronouncement. But I couldn't register their words, with their grim faces and somber tones. Whatever it was couldn't overcome the narrative inside my head. The lines that began with *No* and concluded with *I want to run away. Far away. Now.*

The day before, I had been reading about the tsunami that had devastated the island of Indonesia a year earlier. I read that before the wave hit, all the water had rushed out to sea, leaving a dry floor littered with fish. It must have been an eerie calm, watching, waiting, wondering if the water would return.

After the doctors left the room, I felt like a woman standing on that beach. I didn't believe what was happening, and so I watched, as if it were someone else's life. As if the water would never come back. As if there weren't a tidal wave on its way.

They brought Penny into the room, swaddled tight, her head covered in a blue-and-pink striped hat. All we could see was her little round face. She felt so light as she gazed up at me with those big blue eyes. Her cheeks looked splotchy. When Peter held her, his long arms enveloped her body. He rocked her and stroked her cheek.

As I looked at them together, questions flooded my mind, stealing me from the sweetness of seeing Peter become a father. *How could this happen? What does this mean for her? Will I be able to be proud of her? Will I be able to love her?*

A nurse entered the room and handed me a pamphlet about breast-feeding. I scanned the page. "You may have difficulties," it read, "if your baby is more than three weeks early . . . If your baby weighs less than six pounds . . . If your baby has Down syndrome." It struck me as such a terrible introduction to nursing that I almost laughed out loud. But Penny nestled in and began to eat. It was awkward, and she kept falling asleep, and yet she latched on and sucked. She did it just right. The nurse said, "She's doing better than any other newborn I've seen today."

For the first time since Peter had told me the news, I smiled. And by the time Penny had finished nursing, I heard a whisper of peace. I sat there without words, without tears, looking at her and wondering what lay ahead. Earlier in the day, the epidural had numbed me from the waist down. Now, its effect worn off, I winced with the effort of trying to sit up. But my emotions seemed to have followed my body, as though an anesthesiologist had found a way into my soul, temporarily protecting me from the fear and sadness and guilt.

I was still sitting there, calm and solemn, when my sisters and mother walked in. I had heard them in the hallway, the cheery cadences of their conversation wafting into the room. But they knew as soon as they saw us. And then the first tear trickled down my cheek. I tried to tell them, but I had to wave in Peter's direction. He said it again, "The doctors think Penny has Down syndrome."

Mom nodded, almost as if the news had confirmed a suspicion. Kate's eyes got big. Brooks jerked her head a little, as if she had been slapped. Elly looked at the floor.

"May I hold her?" Mom asked. With Penny in her arms, she said, "I knew something was wrong from the way the nurses were looking at each other after the delivery. They kept catching each other's eyes and trying to catch your doctor's eye, and they weren't smiling. And Penny's body didn't look like all of you when you were born. I wondered if she had dislocated her shoulder or something."

I thought back to Penny naked, her limbs splayed as they washed her after birth. I hadn't seen it then, but Mom was right. Her body had looked different from those classic images of newborns curled up tight, arms and legs pulled in.

"And they took her away so quickly," Mom said. Her voice held relief, as if she had been worried she would return to news far worse.

Again, I hadn't thought anything of the timing. I hadn't held Penny for long, but it hadn't struck me as odd. I just didn't know any better.

A nurse interrupted. "Penny's body temp is on the low side, and we need to run some more tests," she said, extending her arms.

Kate said, "But I haven't gotten to hold her yet."

"I'll bring her back as soon as we're done."

Silence settled upon us once Penny was gone until I said, "I need to call Dad."

"Do you want me to do it?" Peter asked.

I shook my head even though I didn't want to pick up the phone, to call him back, as though I were retracting the good news from a few hours ago.

It was the first time I said it out loud: "The doctors think Penny has Down syndrome."

"Oh," Dad said.

"But she seems healthy," I added.

"Good."

"See you tomorrow?"

"See you tomorrow."

When I had told my family I was pregnant, Dad had jumped up and down in the middle of our living room with exclamations of delight. I had never seen him so happy. "Nancy," he said to my mother, intertwining his fingers with hers, "we're going to be grandparents."

After I hung up the phone, a stone of fear dropped into my stomach. *What if our families don't love her?*

Mom went back to our apartment around ten o'clock, but my sisters waited two more hours until Penny was back in the room. They stroked her cheeks and rocked her and kissed her forehead. Aunt Kate. Aunt Brooks. Aunt Elly. I was the oldest child and the oldest grandchild. Penny was the first daughter, the first niece, the first granddaughter, the first great-granddaughter. And they all wanted to be with her, even though everything I thought we had known about her had been swept away.

By midnight I had been awake for almost twenty-four hours. My sisters said their good-byes. Penny nursed again, and Peter curled up to sleep in the fold-out cot next to my bed, his hand resting upon my thigh.

A nurse came in. She recorded my temperature and my blood pressure and asked about my pain. I handed Penny to her, and she turned to walk out of the room. Almost as an afterthought, she stepped toward me and said, "I had a special child, too."

I couldn't see her face in the dim light. I was lying down, on the edge of sleep.

"How old is your child now?" I asked.

Her tone stayed the same—even and soothing—when she said, "He died a long time ago."

I closed my eyes for a moment. I didn't want it to be true. I said, "I'm sorry."

She looked past me and shook her head, as if I didn't understand. Before she took her leave, she said, "He was a gift."

I am crying because of you. Because of joy and love that run deeper than any logical construction. Because of sorrow that you are not who I thought you would be.

You are beautiful. You are my daughter. We are delighted to meet you.

And yet I cry . . .

I don't want to cry over the birth of my daughter.

January 2006

2

Again and again that night, I emerged from the blissful anonymity of sleep with my heart racing, as if a door had slammed shut, as if a gunshot had pierced the silence. And then I would remember, and I would tell myself, *Your daughter has Down syndrome*, and I would try to figure out how I had come to be this person, this mother.

Peter slept straight through, his body rising and falling in a gentle rhythm. They brought Penny in to nurse, and he hardly stirred. But I stayed awake, gazing at her little round face, trying to make sense of it all. I didn't know much about Down syndrome, but I did know that it had happened at the moment of conception, as soon as the chromosomes from Peter's body joined the ones from mine. From the beginning. Before I even knew she existed.

I thought back to that day in early May. In the course of a week, two friends had called. Each of them said, "I dreamed last night that you were pregnant." And so, on a warm spring morning, I took a test. Peter had been on his way out the door to coach a tennis match, and I had asked, "Could you wait about three minutes?" I didn't tell him why until I emerged from the bathroom wide-eyed, smiling. I held out the pregnancy test with its little blue plus sign. He yelped and wrapped his arms around me.

And here she was, falling asleep against my chest. Here she was, needing me to be her mother. Here she was, beautiful and fragile and not who I had expected. This child who had danced along my spine, slept against my organs, kicked my ribs, and handled my hipbones. This child who had been to places inside me that I had never seen or touched, that I had only begun to feel because of her.

Her hands were so tiny—white fingernails that looked as though she had a manicure in the womb—and a chubby face with an upturned nose and puffy eyes. I gazed at her, and the nurse's words, "He was a gift," came back to me, a simple, haunting refrain.

Peter went out to get coffee in the morning. He returned with a blueberry muffin and a cup of tea just the way I liked it, with one Splenda and a lot of milk. The whole room was a testimony to his care for me—the down comforter and pillow he had brought from home; the laptop computer with speakers set up so I could listen to music; the stack of magazines—*Time, The Atlantic, The New Yorker, First Things*—in case I had needed a diversion during labor; and the pile of pastel-colored baby clothes on the windowsill.

He had put away the sheets and pillows from his own makeshift bed and now he sat next to me, elbows on knees, both hands around the coffee cup, eyes down. I wanted to talk, but I didn't know what to say. The question that repeated itself inside my head was, *How could this happen?* When I tried to come up with an answer, all I could think was, *We haven't done anything to deserve this. We haven't done anything wrong. And Down syndrome is the one thing she can't have, the one thing we ruled out.*

Halfway through my pregnancy, in August, Dr. Mayer had called. Peter and I were on vacation at my family's summer house. It was midafternoon, and we sat side by side in beach chairs overlooking the water. The air was clear enough to see Long Island, miles away. Its sandy beaches were obscured.

Only the trees met my eye, as if they were floating above the water with nothing to anchor them in place.

"I've been trying to track you down," Dr. Mayer said, a hint of admonishment in her voice.

"I'm sorry," I replied. I sat upright, like a kid in school who had been caught not paying attention.

"We got some test results back," she said, more gently. "From the quad screen you had last week. We've been leaving messages at home, but I really needed to get in touch with you."

I moved my sunglasses to the top of my head, as if I could look Dr. Mayer in the eye. Peter put his book aside.

"What is it?" I asked.

"The results show a 1 in 316 chance that your baby has Down syndrome. Technically, that's not considered a risk. One in 250 counts as a risk. But you're so young. For a woman your age, the risk should be closer to 1 in 1,000. You might want to do some follow-up tests."

She went through the options. A definitive answer could only come via an amniocentesis, but it posed a slight risk of miscarriage.

"No," I said. "We don't need that."

Peter and I had already agreed we wouldn't terminate the pregnancy in the event of abnormalities, so we scheduled a Level Two ultrasound one week later. And we rejoiced when the technician reported, "This baby may be many things, but it won't have Down syndrome."

As I looked at Peter huddled over his coffee, I heard his words again, his pronouncement from the night before, *They think she has Down syndrome*. I wanted to summon that ultrasound technician who had measured Penny's femur, her tibia and fibula, the fold of skin at the back of her neck. That woman who had traced Penny's picture on the screen and said, "See, the baby is sucking its thumb." I wanted to summon her and tell her she was wrong. I wanted to say, *It is your fault that we are not prepared. It is your fault that we didn't know.*

But knowledge wouldn't have made a difference. I could never have imagined the words *mental retardation* or *birth defect* being used in the same sentence as my child's name. It was as if having kids had become an equation: youth plus devotion to God plus education equaled a healthy and normal baby. As if taking a birthing class and reading baby books and abstaining from alcohol and praying all guaranteed certain things about our family. As if I were entitled to exactly the baby I had imagined, a little version of myself, a child who was verbally precocious and walked early and went on to skip kindergarten and excel in school. But there I was, in a hospital gown on a Saturday morning, and my child had Down syndrome.

Peter's phone broke the silence. He looked at it and said, "It's my brother." He rubbed his forehead. "I can't answer it. I wouldn't be able to say hello without crying."

Peter's younger brother Christian was at a wedding in New Orleans for one of their cousins. He knew Penny had been born, but he didn't know anything else. Peter glanced at the phone as it rang again. He pushed "Ignore call."

He looked up at me, his voice tight. "I feel like I've been swallowed by darkness. I can't . . ." He shook his head and turned away. "I can't . . ." He didn't finish the sentence.

A nurse brought Penny into the room. She was swaddled tight, and someone had added a large floppy bow to her standard-issue blue-and-pink striped hat. "She's adorable," the nurse said.

"Thank you," I murmured, receiving Penny into my arms.

"I brought you all some information. From the Internet." She handed a small stack of papers to Peter. "And I'm going to try to put you in touch with some other families who've been in the same situation."

"How often does this happen?" I asked.

"You're the third I've known where a Down's baby was born unexpectedly. That's in the past five years. So, not very often."

I worked on the math. *How many babies were born each year in this hospital? Five a day? Ten? Thousands every year. Thousands. And once or twice, with an unknown extra chromosome.*

After the nurse left, I said to Peter, "We've become those people."

"Those people?"

"You know, the exceptional ones."

There were plenty of unusual aspects of our life together—we didn't watch more than an hour a week of television, we were educated and lived in the Northeast *and* believed in Jesus, we had met in high school and dated through college and got married three weeks after graduation. *Exceptional*, I thought, with a hint of bitterness. I looked at Penny again, and the tone of the voice inside my head softened. *Exceptional.*

Peter reached out his arms. "May I?"

She was so little. He held her head in the palm of his hand and tucked her body close to his. Her toes reached the crook of his arm. He wiped his eyes. "Hello, beautiful," he said to her. It was the same way he had greeted me most days of our marriage, and it gave me a glimpse of what I had been hoping for, the chance to meet a new part of my husband once Penny was born. We had waited so long to have children, and we both had feared that a child would change our lives too dramatically. But one thing I had longed for was to see Peter as a father, to see the part of him that only Penny could evoke. I had looked forward to the ways she would give us to one another all over again.

The nurse soon returned for Penny. Her body temperature was still low, and she needed more time under a heat lamp. Peter and I were alone again, by design. My family had agreed to return the next day. We hadn't called any of our friends yet. It was as if we needed to test each other first, to say the words we were thinking and find out if they would disqualify us from our new roles as mother and father.

"I don't want to go back to Lawrenceville," Peter said.

"Me neither."

I closed my eyes. I wanted to run away. I had visions of putting Penny in her car seat and heading north to my parents' summer house. I knew the route well: up the turnpike and over the George Washington Bridge, onto the Henry Hudson and into Connecticut and finally, off the highway and onto a narrow road that wound its way back toward the water. Past the year-round residences and around the bend, the salt marsh in front of us. Into the driveway, up a small hill, and then seeing the Sound. The choppy gray water. The solitude. The open space.

"But we have to go back," I said out loud.

Peter paced the room. His eyes darted from chair to corner to bed to door, as if he were looking for a place to settle his gaze, as if he were looking for some stable point in a world that had just started to float away. "I don't want to be ashamed of her," he said. He stopped walking and hung his head.

I thought of him holding her. *Hello, beautiful.*

"You're going to be a wonderful father."

He shook his head, not quite in disagreement. More with helplessness, or despair. "I'm just so afraid."

I had tried to sound positive, but I was swimming through the same thoughts—*What do we do with a child who is mentally retarded? What if people think this is our fault? What if they pity us? What will it take for us to be able to care for her?*

I finally said, "I think I could have handled it if she weren't our first child, if I'd had time to learn how to be a mom and how to raise a baby. But this . . ." I clutched the folds of my hospital gown and then smoothed it out over my torso. "This just seems impossible."

Peter's phone interrupted us again. It was his brother Christian, the third time.

"He's like a dog with a bone," Peter said.

"He loves you," I replied. "I think you need to tell him."

"Hello?" Peter answered. "Yeah, I did get your messages. Look, this is hard to say. I didn't want to tell you in the middle of the wedding and everything. But the thing is . . ." He looked at me and took a deep breath. "She has Down syndrome. The doctors think Penny has Down syndrome." Christian said something in response, and the tears ran down Peter's cheeks, and I remembered hearing that tears released toxins from our bodies, that tears brought healing.

Peter said, "I'm sorry to tell you. That's why I wasn't answering your calls. I knew I couldn't fake it once we talked." He was silent. "Thanks. I love you, man."

I had never seen Peter like this before. He had weathered his mother's death a few years earlier. He had wept over the loss of a friend in a car accident. But even then, his hopeful attitude shone. It was a running joke, and a running point of contention, that he was the optimist and I was, by my reckoning, the realist in our marriage. He always looked on the bright side. He always assumed it would work out, whatever it might be. But the lines on his face, the rigidity of his body, the forced smiles and eyes that looked away as quickly as possible—I had never seen this before. I felt as though all morning I had been watching him in a fistfight, a blow to the jaw and then a punch to the stomach until he was on the ground, curled in a ball, quiet and still.

And so I had to ask the question. "Do you still want to name her Penny?"

His face softened. "Of course I do."

It had seemed such a perfect choice, to name her after her grandmother, Peter's mom, who had died just two years earlier. On the day the ultrasound technician shared the news that our child didn't have Down syndrome, she also had written the baby's gender on a scrap of paper, per our request. We had opened the note in the parking lot, sitting side by side in the car, Peter's hand upon my belly. I read out loud, "Buy pink! It's a girl!"

A few minutes later I had asked, "Do you know what you want to name her?"

"I think I'm biased," he replied.

"I think I have the same bias."

She was Penny from that moment on. And throughout the pregnancy we compared her to her grandmother. When she fluttered her legs in the womb, we talked about her namesake's love of dancing, her desire for attention, her spunkiness, her sass. We talked about her beauty, that people regularly compared her to Natalie Wood or Elizabeth Taylor. We had expected our Penny to be similar to her grandmother. But now I wasn't so sure.

There was another knock on the door, and Dr. Mayer walked in. Her cautious smile and curly brown hair, her understated presence—her whole demeanor made me think of my mother. She pressed my belly. Her hands reminded me that my body was recovering from trauma. I closed my eyes against the pain.

"How does it feel?" she asked.

"It's not so bad."

"You didn't have much tearing. You should heal in no time."

In no time. I tried to smile. "Thanks."

Dr. Mayer pulled up a chair. "How are you?"

My eyes searched the room for a minute, then finally landed on my hands. At first, all I could think about was practicing the piano as a little girl, with my long fingers stretching for the proper configurations, reaching, pounding my fists into the keys when I couldn't get it right. I shook my head. "I feel fine," I said, gesturing toward my body, as if she were asking about my physical state.

Maybe my response was a test. And if it was, she passed, because she didn't take it as a cue to leave. Instead she said, "I have three kids. But I had a fourth, a baby who miscarried. And that baby had Down syndrome."

I looked her in the eye then, even though I could feel my emotions rising. "How did you know that Penny had Down syndrome?"

"I didn't. The neonatologist called me out of the room, and even then I didn't believe her. She had to convince me."

"Well then, how did she know?"

"Babies with Down syndrome have low muscle tone, hypotonia. And an extra fold of skin over their eyes. And Penny has a line across her palm that you won't find without that extra chromosome."

"So now you're sure?" I asked, realizing that there was still a part of me that hoped someone would come in and tell us it all had been a horrible mistake.

"You can't be sure until you get a karyotype. For most people with Down syndrome, there's an extra chromosome in every cell of the body. But sometimes that extra chromosome is only in certain cells. That's called Mosaic Down syndrome. Penny's so healthy, it could be that."

Peter said, "I'm confused. If we can't know for sure, what are we supposed to tell people?"

"I'd say something along the lines of, 'It is very likely that Penny will have special needs as the result of a chromosomal abnormality.'"

Peter reached for a pen. "Can you say that again?" He mouthed the words as he wrote them, rehearsing.

Dr. Mayer's pager beeped, and she silenced it without taking her eyes off my face. "You all are going to be fine," she said. "You have a strong marriage and a strong faith and a beautiful baby."

As soon as she left the room, Peter began a series of calls—to his best friend, Daniel, and then his father, his aunts, his college roommates. He held the notepad with the doctor's words. *It is very likely . . .*

With each call, he seemed to gain confidence. His face softened. His shoulders dropped. When he hung up the phone I was nursing Penny again, tapping her cheek with my fingernail to keep her awake.

"I have prayed for so many years that my heart would become more open," Peter said. He leaned close to Penny and whispered, "Maybe you are an answer to prayer, little one."

Penny stayed with us for the rest of the afternoon and into the evening. Mostly, she slept. But every so often she pushed her warm face into my chest and nestled in to nurse. And she opened her eyes, her fascinating eyes, like pools in shadows with points of light gleaming through. We laughed that afternoon, when she crinkled her forehead in alarm or looked around the room with a mischievous expression. When she was in our arms, it felt like it had when I was pregnant. Simple love. Abundant love. The complications dropped away.

The only call I made was to our pastor. I was in my second year of seminary, and as a part of my degree, I had been working as an intern in our church. I wanted people to start praying for us. I needed people to start praying for us.

Pastor Mike answered on the third ring. I told him the news, and at first I found myself forcing cheer: "She's really healthy and she's nursing well, so those are good things." But then I realized he was crying.

Just a few weeks earlier, I had preached a short sermon on the Christmas carol "Joy to the World." I focused on "Let every heart prepare him room," and I talked about preparing room for Jesus in our hearts and lives this Christmas season. I described the preparations we had made for Penny—baby showers and maternity clothes and installing the car seat. That sermon had made me think about Mary preparing to welcome Jesus, and it had prompted me to pray that God would prepare me to receive Penelope. But we hadn't been prepared at all.

I said to Pastor Mike, "It's been really hard." I looked over at Peter holding Penny. "But this afternoon has been better."

"It's like a crucifixion and resurrection all at once," Pastor Mike said.

When I hung up the phone, I reached for Penny. I pulled her hand out from the swaddling blankets and traced the line on her palm, the strong horizontal line that stretched from one side to the other. I compared her hand to mine, noting the distinction. And I wondered, as I rubbed her soft skin, *What does this line tell us about the road ahead?*

I don't know how to think about the fallen-ness of creation, the "groaning." Or how to think about extra chromosomes. Could Adam and Eve have had a Down syndrome baby? Is it part of the fall or just our reaction? Maybe her body is no less fallen than mine, and I just see it on a continuum that doesn't exist in God's economy. I am reminded of Flannery O'Connor's characters, people as sacraments, visible reminders of God's grace. Visible brokenness that only helps us understand who we all are—broken yet beloved.

January 2006

3

It was Sunday, January 1. I rubbed the sleep from my eyes. The first thing I saw, perched on my bedside table, was a bottle of champagne. My sisters had arrived with it two days earlier, and we planned to open it all together. But then the euphoria had slipped away. I had slept better that second night in the hospital, and I was starting to adjust to the idea of a daughter with Down syndrome, but I turned my head from the champagne. I wasn't ready to celebrate.

I pushed the bed into an upright position and scanned my body, surprised, somewhat alarmed, to note that I still looked pregnant. Until then it had been a relief to wake up and see my round belly. Throughout the recent months I had dreamed, repeatedly, that Penny had died. I woke up frantic every time, but then I would run my hands over my smooth, solid midsection to reassure myself of her presence. And now she was here. Alive. Healthy. I tried to focus my attention on those adjectives as I eased my way out of bed and shuffled to the bathroom. When I returned, I said to Peter, "I want to get dressed."

He helped me out of the hospital gown and into gray sweatpants and a maternity top. Once I had eased myself into the chair next to the bed, Peter leaned over and gave me a kiss. "I'm going to go peek in on Penny," he said.

I nodded and picked up the stack of information the nurse had given us the day before. The first page held the title, "A

Promising Future Together." I read, "*There will be challenges in raising your child, but there will also be many, many joys.*" I appreciated the sentiment, but it seemed vague in comparison to the chart a few pages later that stated a list of areas in which Penny's development would be delayed: sitting, crawling, standing, walking, talking, smiling, eating, potty-training. Or the list of potential medical concerns: cardiac problems, cataracts, hearing loss.

Whoever had written these pages had been careful with their language. They called it trisomy 21 because it is the result of an extra copy of chromosome 21. They called children like Penny "children with Down syndrome," not "Down's children," and exhorted me to "remember that Down syndrome is a condition your baby has, it is not who your baby is." I thought about the freedom I felt simply from dressing like a person instead of a patient. It struck me that I needed to make that shift for Penny, too. I needed to start seeing her as our little girl, not as a diagnosis, not as an obstacle to be overcome.

I flipped through the pages, but I didn't get very far. Usually when I was in unknown territory, information settled me, but now it was as if I was looking over my shoulder, waiting for someone to call me back home. I didn't want to be familiar with this landscape yet.

I thought back to the night before, when a nurse had come in. "The cardiologist is here. He needs to do a few tests."

Her words had sent a chill through my body. It was Saturday, December 31. New Year's Eve. And this nurse was telling me we couldn't wait any longer to examine Penny's heart.

"It will take a while, but we'll let you know what he finds out as soon as he's done."

After she wheeled Penny away, Peter crawled into the hospital bed. We curled on our sides, his arms around me. I listened to his steady breathing as he slipped into sleep, but I lay awake. I knew so little. The nurse's words had reminded me that infants with Down syndrome often had heart defects, and I vaguely remembered that they also had a short life expectancy. Exhaustion tried to quiet my thoughts, but soon my heart started to pound. *What if she doesn't make it through the night?*

At that moment I realized, with a measure of relief, I was terrified Penny would die. I was terrified we might lose her. And that fear meant I loved her already. The thought allowed me to slide into sleep until the nurse tapped me on the shoulder.

"Your daughter's heart is fine," she said. "I thought you would want to know."

Twelve hours later, with Peter down the hall checking in on our baby girl, I felt another wave of relief. *She's healthy*, I told myself again and again.

When Peter returned, he looked more like himself—energetic, with bright eyes and a hint of a smile. "She is so tiny," he said. "They've put this ten-pounder next to her in the nursery. I swear he's a football player already! And they said she can come in here soon."

"Do you know anyone with Down syndrome?" I asked.

He paused for a moment. "I did growing up. George Williams. Blake's little brother. I didn't know him well or anything. I think he died." Peter looked at me, taking in the signs that I was deep in thought—arms crossed, forehead creased, biting the inside of my lip. "Why do you ask?"

"I don't know anyone with Down syndrome. And this website says there are 350,000 in the United States. Which means . . ." I sighed. "Which means I've somehow missed this whole group of people."

He sat down on the side of the bed, facing me. "And?"

"Well, what does that say about me?"

"It says . . ." He tapped his fingers together. "I don't know what it says."

"It says I've either ignored or avoided a whole group of people for my entire life. I've been thinking about our families. Kate had Mandy, her Best Buddy in college, remember?

Mandy had Down syndrome. They got together every week for dinner. Kate loved her so much. She said Mandy was the best thing about her freshman year. And then Brooks volunteered at that orphanage in Peru, and her favorite kid was a kid with Down syndrome. I remember the pictures. And Elly was a Best Buddy in college, too. But I always thought that people with disabilities just weren't my thing. I'm so ignorant." I lay my head against the back of the chair and stared at the ceiling. "No, it's more than that. I feel like I've never had time to even acknowledge these people's existence, much less to actually get to know them."

Peter walked over and knelt down next to the chair so that he was looking in my eyes. "Age," he said, "don't beat yourself up. What good will that do?"

"Even your dad knows more about special needs than we do." I intended to argue my point, but the thought brought a smile to my face. Peter's father worked as a regular substitute teacher these days, and one of his favorite assignments was kids with disabilities. He was from Denmark, and even though he had been in America for over thirty years, he still mixed up words occasionally. The last time we were together, he told us, "I particularly enjoy the acoustic children." He had meant autistic. We all giggled, but I had been struck by the sincerity of his statement.

Peter squeezed my hand. "The bottom line is that we've got a lot to learn."

He was talking about abstract knowledge, of course, but we also found ourselves ignorant about the most basic tasks. Bathing. Swaddling. Rocking her to sleep. The nurses made it look so easy. Peter and I held Penny as if she were a china doll that might shatter at any moment. They handled her more like a loaf of bread.

"Do you want to go see her?" Peter asked, and I realized I hadn't left the room yet. He held my elbow as we walked down the hall. We entered the nursery, and I scanned the rows of clear plastic containers holding other newborns until I landed on Penny, flat on her back wearing only her diaper, tongue sticking out of her mouth. She turned her head toward her dad. He leaned close and stuck his tongue out in return.

We started asking questions, and soon enough a nurse was teaching us to bathe Penny with cotton balls, swabbing the soapy water under her neck, her armpits, running it across her chest and face. "Just make sure she doesn't get too cold," the nurse said. She fastened a new diaper in place and swaddled her tight. "Do you have some clothes for when she goes home?"

"My mom's going to bring some preemie clothes," I said, thinking back to the pile of outfits we had brought with us to the hospital. All of them had seemed tiny. But none of them would fit until Penny had gained three or four pounds, almost doubling her body weight.

Everyone in my family was due to return that day. Kate arrived first, her long blond hair swept back in a ponytail, no makeup, red eyes. Suddenly I felt like an older sister again, as she brushed away another tear with the back of her hand. I stood to greet her with a long hug.

After a loud exhale, Kate squared her shoulders and said, "Mom and Dad will be here soon. They're just parking the car. How's Penny?"

"She's great," I said as we both sat down. I pulled my legs toward my chest. "They say her heart is fine and her temperature is starting to get more stable. And she's nursing well. She's great."

"How are you?"

"Better," I said, realizing as I spoke that it was true. I hadn't cried much the day before. Those hours had held a frightening calm, like the eye of a hurricane. It was different now. The calm felt peaceful, not ominous. "I think we're going to be fine. I'm starting to learn about Down syndrome"—I motioned to the papers nearby—"and Peter's doing a lot better. . . ." I trailed off.

"You're crazy," she said. Her tone was gentle, with a hint of humor. "I spent the whole day crying yesterday. I cried the whole ride down here. And here you are in real clothes, acting so normal, like having a Down syndrome baby is no big deal."

I shrugged. Kate knew me well enough to understand that I had to think for a while before I would be able to feel much of anything. More tears would come, and probably some anger and hurt and guilt and fear. I could predict the emotions, but I couldn't access them. For now, I had to work it out in my head. I had to construct a plan. And I needed some answers. Some of my questions were practical. The pediatrician had said Penny would need physical therapy—*How do we set that up? Will insurance pay for it?* And I wanted to meet all the other Down's babies—or, as the information packet would have it, babies with Down syndrome—in the area. *Where were they?* And then there were the health concerns. *How would we find the right doctors? Who would check her hearing and her eyesight and everything else?*

There was another set of questions, questions that weren't so easily answered by phone calls or a reference book. I hadn't realized it until we received Penny's diagnosis, but I had come into the hospital with a grid that ordered my sense of how the world worked. I believed that all people were created in the image of God, that every human being bore the mark of God's goodness and light. But I also believed that everything that went wrong in the world was a consequence of sin. I didn't think that God was doling out tornados or cancer or malaria as punishment for us doing bad things or something like that. I just believed that ultimately all the pain and injustice in the world could be traced back, somehow, to the human refusal to love God. The first human choice of self over God sent suffering and discord everywhere, like a fault line tearing through the universe.

Before Penny was born, I would have assumed that an extra chromosome was just that, a crack in the cosmos, evidence of the fractured nature of all creation. But how could I imagine such a thing about my daughter? I couldn't figure it out.

I didn't have time to try to articulate my thoughts. Peter wheeled Penny back in just as Mom and Dad walked through the door. She was fast asleep and swaddled tight. They crowded around. Her skin was smooth now, with a hint of olive underneath her pink cheeks. Peter picked her up and handed her to Dad. "Here you go, Grandpa."

On the surface, we were introducing the firstborn grandchild to her grandfather. Big smiles. *Oohs* and *aahs* about how cute she was. But there was an undercurrent of hesitation. *How do we say* Congratulations *and* I'm sorry? *How do we celebrate and grieve at the same moment?*

Dad lowered himself into a chair with Penny. I couldn't remember seeing him with an infant before. He held his body stiffly, shoulders hunched, using only his arms to hold her. He looked the same as ever—khakis, loafers, a button-down shirt with a frayed collar, a blue wool sweater with a few stains. But I had to wonder if he would become someone different now that he was a grandfather. Now that Penny was his granddaughter. She slept without stirring, and he smiled.

A new nurse walked in and started talking to Mom. "Can you tell Penny's mom that Penny's bilirubin level is still higher than we want? That's why she looks a little jaundiced. But as long as it stays where it is, we're in good shape."

Mom interrupted. "Um, Penny's mom is right here." She pointed to me.

"Oh!" the nurse said to me. "I'm sorry. You look so comfortable for a woman who just gave birth. I thought you were one of the sisters. I heard there were a lot of them."

"Two more on the way," I said.

"How's your pain?" the nurse asked.

Labor and delivery had been a lot easier than I had expected. "I've been taking the Motrin and using ice packs. It's really not that bad."

Kate said, "She comes from a long line of stoic New England women."

The nurse gave a short laugh. "All right. Well, call if you need me."

Soon we were sharing memories of the past few days, as if they had happened a long time ago. Mom talked again about how she had known something was wrong, how Penny had looked so floppy on the examining table. Kate mentioned her tears. Dad said he hadn't been able to sleep on Friday night. "I've got a cold sore," he noted, pointing to a bump on his lip.

I felt a strange urge to apologize, although I knew that none of them were looking for consolation, especially not from me. With Penny in the room, beautiful, peaceful, there was also a sense that it had been a false alarm, that all the fear and stress and sadness was for nothing.

Kate went over to Dad and said, "All right, Grandpa, hand her over." She put her face close to Penny and bumped noses. After she sat down, she said, "Did any of you hear them on Friday night in the room next door?"

I had a vague recollection of shouts of praise through the wall.

"Yeah," Peter said. "They had a baby girl a few hours after Penny."

"But did you hear what they said?" Kate asked. "It was right after we'd gotten back from dinner. I walked into this room to see Age crying, and I knew there was something wrong. And just a few minutes after you told us, there was all this happy shouting next door. I heard someone say, 'She's perfect! She's perfect!' over and over. It was so weird."

I hadn't heard those exclamations. I looked at Penny in Kate's arms. All the medical terminology implied anything but perfection. *Birth defect. Chromosomal abnormality.*

Kate bumped Penny's nose with her own again and gave her a kiss.

"What I want to figure out is whether Down syndrome is a mistake," I said. "I know that scientists and doctors would say that it is." I gestured toward the papers on the table. "But how do I think about it in terms of God? Is it a manifestation of sin in the world? Is Penny less perfect than that little girl who was born next door?"

The room stayed silent. I thought back to the moment I first felt Penny kick. We were in Rome, living in a dorm room. Peter was there on a Fulbright scholarship with twenty other high school teachers. At least once each night I got out of our bed and walked across the linoleum floor to the communal bathroom. One of those nights, in mid-July, I couldn't fall back to sleep. And that's when I first felt her move. A flutter below my belly button. And then another. And three more. *Hello, little one.*

How could she be a mistake?

I looked up when Mom spoke in her gentle, level voice. "The only evidence of sin that I see in Penny's birth is in how we respond to her."

It was as if I had been looking through a kaleidoscope and it turned a notch. All the same pieces and parts, the same colors even, but a totally new pattern. A new way of seeing.

For the first time in months, I remembered those words in the car before Penny was born. *But if you had waited, then you wouldn't have had* this *child.*

This child.

PART TWO

whoever receives this child, receives me

Consciously and unconsciously, we had implicit hopes, dreams, and expectations for Penny that having Down syndrome makes unlikely. At the same time, we didn't want to be upset in any way concerning the birth of our daughter. We also realized that it was hardest to deal with this new reality when Penny wasn't in the room with us. When she was out of the room, she became an abstract concept. When she was in the room—nursing, sleeping, just being held—she became who she is: our beautiful, sweet daughter. The more time we spent with her, the more pure joy we experienced. Who knows what the days and years ahead will hold, but one thing we know for certain: We could not be happier that Penny is our daughter.

From a letter by Peter, January 2006

4

"They really trust us to take care of a baby?" Peter asked.

"People do this every day," I said. "Girls half my age. Besides, we have my mother to help."

Penny lay in my arms, asleep again. She looked like a cherub, pudgy cheeks and a button nose and gentle breaths that moved her chest up and down. Mom and Dad had brought preemie clothes, and the warm white of her pajamas made her skin glow.

It was Sunday night, only forty-eight hours after giving birth. I was sore, but Motrin eased the pain. I could walk, get dressed, take a shower. Penny's body temperature was stable. At five pounds, her weight was stable, too. She was small, and she had Down syndrome, but she was as healthy as could be. It was time to go home.

Penny slept through her introduction to our apartment. She didn't stir as her aunts and grandparents gathered around. She didn't notice when I picked up our cat, George, and let him study her face. The flash of the camera didn't wake her when it captured our first family photo—Peter cradling Penny, me with George slung over my shoulder, three times her size.

Peter, Mom, and Dad moved toward the kitchen to work on dinner. My sisters followed me into Penny's room. I scrolled through my memory, looking for a file marked *bedtime*. Penny had taken a bath at the hospital. She had a clean diaper. She was already wearing pajamas. It didn't make any sense to read a book. A song. That was it. We would sing her a song.

As kids, Mom sang to us every night before we went to sleep. Each of us had our own lullaby, and I wanted to sing mine to Penny. We summoned Mom to lead us, as none of us could remember the words. What I could remember was the comfort of Mom sitting next to me on the bed as a child, singing softly with the lights out, her hand resting upon my shoulder.

All four of us chimed in at parts as Mom sang, "Close your eyes, close your eyes, go to sleep now, my darling . . ."

I kissed Penny's forehead and placed her in a Moses basket. She lay still, bundled tight. I placed my hand on her chest once again, soothed by the steadiness of her breathing.

As we tiptoed out of the room, Kate said, "Of course, I'm not sure why we did that, since Pen was asleep the whole time."

Kate giggled as soon as she said it, and I laughed out loud. Mom turned around with a smile, and pretty soon I was laughing the way I had as a little girl, when the four of us sat between Mom and Dad at family dinners and couldn't contain our emotions. And just like those days when I was nine or ten, as soon as my laughter ebbed, I looked at Kate, saw her nostrils flare as she tried to contain giggles, and lost it once again. I wiped tears from my eyes and took a deep breath.

Before joining the family in the kitchen, I peeked in on Penny once more.

Go to sleep now, my darling.

A few hours later, Peter and I climbed into bed. I leaned back against a bank of pillows. My eyes wandered, resting on familiar objects as if to ensure I had truly made it home. Glimpses of our life together. The photo of Peter and me in front of the Louvre. The sturdy, weathered dresser that a friend had given us when we lived in Richmond. The framed poem Peter's college roommate had written for us when we got married. The quilt of fabrics from Peter's mother's wardrobe.

George jumped up and peered into Penny's basket, which we had placed on a table at the end of the bed. I moved onto my hands and knees to join him. There was our new addition. Our daughter.

For a moment it all seemed so right. So easy. A mother and father come home with a beautiful, healthy baby girl. To the cheers of aunts and proud grandparents. To a jealous cat. To a yellow room with a cozy armchair and a stack of novels to read while nursing and blankets and toys and clothes and everything else a baby could ever want.

But we were also coming home to a dorm that housed thirty boys—thirty boys who would return from vacation the next day. We were coming home to Peter's colleagues, teachers, men and women with multiple advanced degrees, men and women like us who would cringe at the words *mental retardation*.

Peter had brought his laptop to bed. "I need to write a letter to the faculty," he said.

"What are you going to tell them?"

"I'm going to tell them as much as we know. I don't want rumors. I don't want anyone to think we're in denial. I don't want anyone to think we're trying to hide."

"I hate the feeling that there's a caveat when we announce the birth of our daughter."

Peter started to type. I didn't lie down yet, but I closed my eyes.

Until that point, boarding school life had seemed normal. Peter and I had met at a boarding school, and now we lived at one—Lawrenceville. Students from across the country and around the globe came here, lived here, in order to receive the best education possible. They would all go to college, and many of them would go on to have distinguished careers in finance or medicine or the arts. *How does Penny fit into this place?*

I glanced at Peter's letter.

Our daughter, Penny Becker, was born on Friday evening. Penny is a beautiful little girl and the apple of her father's eye.

A beautiful little girl.

She was beautiful. But she also looked different. Mom had seen it immediately. The doctors could list all her distinguishing features. Her beauty was unconventional. The type of beauty I had rarely been able to see.

When Peter and I were in school, everyone had taken a poll for the yearbook and voted on which senior girl was the best looking. A friend of mine held the honor. After she was announced the winner, she almost dropped out of school, almost didn't make it through the spring. I don't know what triggered it exactly, but she started losing weight in January, and a few pounds became ten, then twenty, until her clothes hung off her body, the structure of her face became pronounced, and her collarbones jutted out of her shoulders.

She wasn't alone. I spent those high school years saying that I didn't care how I looked. I didn't wear makeup or do anything to my hair, and I only took a shower when it seemed absolutely necessary. But the thought of gaining even one pound left me panicked. I found a journal from my sophomore year that recorded my eating patterns on a typical day: Apple. Salad. Frozen Yogurt. Apple. Diet Coke. It recorded exercise, too: Three mile run. Ninety-minute soccer practice. Thirty minutes on the stationary bike. Fifty sit-ups. The same journal contained a vow I had written to myself: "I pledge that I will not eat more than 1,000 calories per day." It was signed and dated. A covenant with the gods of thinness, the currency of beauty.

The pledge to starve myself hadn't lasted very long. A few months, and then I went home for Christmas break and couldn't keep it up. Mom cooked dinner, so I had to either feign illness or eat. The odd thing was, when I started eating again, my body rejected the food. I didn't make myself throw up. It just happened, as if the food had nowhere to go.

I told Mom about this strange sickness, and once the hubbub of Christmas had passed, we went to the doctor. A series of tests ensued until finally, six weeks later, after I had lost fifteen of my 102 pounds, doctors diagnosed me with *gastro paresis*, paralysis of the stomach. It took six more years before I ate healthily again.

The girls at Lawrenceville reminded me of myself in high school. Lots of energy and drive. A willingness, even eagerness, to address serious intellectual issues. An ability to argue a point. Grades and SAT scores that were higher than the boys'. And a fixation on thinness. It was rare to see anyone on this campus who was overweight.

Just like those girls, I'd always valued thinness and conventional notions of beauty even though I told myself it was shallow, even though I had prayed over the years to be able to see the world differently. I remembered one week in college, in the midst of one of those prayer bouts, when I was able to look at Janet, a girl in my English class, and see that the sweetness of her spirit made her beautiful. Or Ashley, down the hall, with the short brown hair and pocked face and glasses. I noticed the gracefulness of her hands.

But it didn't last long, that ability to see.

And here at Lawrenceville, looking good mattered just as much as it had when I was in high school. Penny already looked different. Almond-shaped eyes. Flat facial features. Tiny ears. Penny looked different, and she was beautiful. *Could Lawrenceville see it? Could Lawrenceville see her? Could I?*

"I'm going to ask Chris to read this to the faculty when they meet in the morning," Peter said, placing the laptop on my outstretched legs.

I read out loud:

"Hi Lawrenceville friends,

Our daughter, Penny, was born on Friday evening. Penny is a beautiful little girl and the apple of her father's eye. But there is more to the story than we first thought. About two hours after Penny came into the world, the doctors told us she is going to have special needs related to a chromosomal abnormality, Down syndrome. Needless to say, this news was utterly shocking to us and we are still (and will be for a long time to come) adjusting to this new reality.

On the one hand, Penny is a beautiful baby who is very healthy, especially for an infant with Down syndrome—her heart is strong, her intestines are working well, and she loves her mother's milk. On the other hand, the future is going to look a lot different than we thought it would, and there is very real grief associated with that. The Lawrenceville community has always comforted and supported us when we've needed it in the past, and we are so glad that this will be Penny's home. Our hope and prayer is that she will be as much of a blessing to this community as we know you will be to her. We sincerely look forward to seeing you all and reentering life here, and we thank you in advance for your thoughts and prayers. It has been a real comfort to be surrounded by family and friends these last two days, so please don't be strangers.

Love,
Peter and Amy Julia"

"It's perfect," I said, handing back the laptop and pulling the covers to my chin. Peter had such faith in this place, these people. But there was so much in me that doubted. So much that feared.

Peter squeezed my leg. "They're going to love her," he said.

I kept my eyes closed for a minute, but then I pushed myself up. No words needed. Just a kiss good-night and my cheek resting against his chest. And then sleep.

We had fun that night. Penny woke me with little grunts every two or three hours. I nudged Peter awake, and together we pulled back the comforter, lay a towel on the bed, and began the process of changing her diaper.

"Why did this look so easy in the hospital?" Peter asked as his big fingers fumbled with the tabs.

"Because the nurses know what they're doing," I said.

As soon as he had the diaper secure, just as I was sliding Penny's arms back into her pajamas, we heard it. Another diaper needed.

I was leaning over to get more supplies when I heard Peter cry out.

"What?"

"She peed on me." At first he sounded puzzled, but soon his face spread into a smile. "And somehow, this little creature managed to pee on her pajamas and the towel, too."

I handed over the new diaper, shaking my head.

Penny blinked at us, serene.

This is good, I thought.

In fits and starts, we were settling into a rhythm of care. We were beginning to learn our daughter.

The next day was more of the same. Try to keep her awake while she nurses. Cycle through as many diapers as it takes to keep her clean and dry. Remember to take Motrin. But mostly, watch as people come to meet her. Peter's brother Christian and his wife, Jennifer, spent the day with us, and Kate's fiancé, Frank, drove down. Penny slept through it all, cuddled in the arms of one of her relatives, and even though she hardly opened her eyes, her presence brought peace.

Lines on Christian's face softened with her in his arms. Dad's shoulders relaxed. Somber tones became spirited, and by the afternoon, the joy in the apartment was palpable.

I still had so many questions, but I was able to hold them at bay. Or perhaps the presence of our family held them at bay. Carried us.

The day wore on, and we could hear doors slamming, feet trudging along the upstairs hallway. The rest of the house began to wake up as the boys returned. I usually welcomed those signs of their presence, but I didn't want to see them yet. I felt safe within the walls of our apartment, with only our family around. I couldn't imagine walking out that door with the eyes of sixteen-year-olds on me. It would be like running through town wearing only a towel. Exposed. Vulnerable.

At nine o'clock that night, Mom and I sat in the living room of our apartment with the door open. The rest of the family had departed, and Peter had gathered the boys for a house meeting in the common room downstairs. I could envision them—a few propped against the pool table, some sitting on the floor, others lounging along the window seat. The jet-lagged ones from Korea and Japan blinking to keep their eyes open. The cool kids raising eyebrows at each other in subtle signs of hello from across the room. Complaining about being back. Happy to be back.

The room quieted, and just a few seconds later, Mom and I heard cheers. Whoops and hollers and applause. Peter had told them that Penny was here. But then the room settled down again. I could guess his next sentence: "Boys, there's more to the story." And I could picture him there—sitting on the arm of a chair so he could see them all, elbows on his knees, hands moving to illustrate his point. I could imagine him telling them all about it. About the doctors' words. About his own tears and fears. About Down syndrome. And then, about Penny. His love for her. The way her presence made him want to dance. He was inviting them into our story.

Thirty minutes passed, and then the cheers rose again, up the stairwell and into our living room, welcoming our daughter into the world.

The days feel like a spiral, where I circle around to sadness or delight or confusion and disbelief. And I know it is ground I have already covered, but I have to go back and scope out the territory again, settle into the landscape, assess the contours of the horizon, try to put one foot in front of the other and move forward. Try to think it will not always come back to fear and sorrow, but that we will circle around until their time is done and we truly can accept this new life as ours, as our family, as normal for us . . .

January 2006

5

The cheers of the boys in our house set the tone. Within hours of sending an email to family and friends that explained the likelihood that Penny would have "special needs," calls and cards and gifts and flowers poured in. One friend hand-delivered a high-tech jogging stroller. A woman from church called to say that we would receive three meals a week until the end of February. One of Peter's colleagues volunteered to teach a class for him through the rest of the winter term. Throughout the month of January, gifts arrived from around the globe—Denmark, England, Mexico, Korea. Penny received seventeen blankets—pink cashmere, light pink fleece, dark pink fleece with PTB embroidered in the corner. Four silver spoons. Eleven bouquets of flowers.

I kept wondering whether people were rejoicing with us in the birth of our firstborn child, or consoling us because she had Down syndrome, or simply doing the best they could to demonstrate their love and support. Or all of the above. I wasn't even sure what I wanted, celebration or sympathy.

And then there was the orchid, which arrived in the middle of our first week home. Two stalks with six blossoms each, all a deep fuchsia. George nudged them with his head and batted his paws at the swaying petals, but there was strength within their delicate construction. It was gorgeous. Over-the-top. A picture of abundance, of life. I was inclined to take it as a sign, a promise.

The gift came from the mother of one of the boys in our house. She couldn't have known that Penny's namesake loved orchids, that her house in New Orleans had been filled with them when she died. She couldn't have known that before Penny was born, my friend Virginia had sent a gift with a quote from Psalm 1: "*Penelope Truesdell Becker, like a tree planted by streams of water, which yields its fruit in season and whose leaf does not wither.*" She couldn't have known how much I hoped, even though I couldn't have said it out loud, that Penny would grow up to be strong, and delicate, and beautiful.

We also received a series of cards—advice, comfort, congratulations. I felt relieved when I read the words "*I don't know what to say.*" But others wrote, "*All parents go through uncertainty and fear when a child is born,*" or, "*She's not really that different.*" It was then that I wanted to protest. They hadn't cried in the hospital. They hadn't come home with information on support groups and questions about life expectancy. They didn't need to report back for a blood draw on the fifth day of their baby's life. They didn't have the pediatrician calling daily, just to check in.

But plenty of people could relate to the sweetness of rocking a baby to sleep or the warmth of a baby's soft skin against their own. Or the nervous energy of all the firsts: the first diaper, the first night home, the first weight check, the first bath.

On Monday, our second evening with Penny in the apartment, Peter and I lay her on a towel on the floor of her room with a space heater nearby. She stretched her scrawny arms and kicked her legs. Since she slept almost all the time in those early days, it was a rare treat to find her wide awake, staring at us and starting to respond to our faces. She puffed out her cheeks and wrinkled her forehead and went through what seemed like a repertoire of tricks. We laughed and I jumped up to get the camera to capture her potbelly and golden skin.

Plenty of people could relate to the love we felt for her.

At the end of that first bath, Mom brought me the phone. I handed Penny to her in return. "It's Virginia," she said.

I dried my hands. "Hello?"

There was no answer.

"Hello?"

I heard something muffled, and I finally realized she was crying. I wished I could reach out my hand and cover the hundreds of miles between us. We had moved to Lawrenceville from Richmond two years earlier, but Virginia was still the first person I had thought to call in the hospital. "Oh, Virginia," I said. "We're okay."

She still didn't respond.

"Penny's doing well. She's healthy and we're happy and it's all good."

I could almost see her nodding and wiping away the tears and swallowing back her emotions. She said, "We were on vacation with my family. I just got home and got your messages. I'm so mad that I was away when this happened. I'm so sorry."

It was as if I were talking to myself a few days earlier, when anger and grief and shock were the only possibilities. All those things were still present, they just had started to be knit together with joy and pride and love and laughter.

"How are you?" she asked.

"I'm doing well. Labor was pretty easy. I took a walk outside today. And nursing doesn't hurt, either. Actually, you'd probably hate me if Penny didn't have Down syndrome."

She tried to laugh. But she knew, and I knew, that she wasn't asking about my body.

"I can tell people are praying for us," I said. "In some ways, it feels like it did after Jack died." A few years earlier, Virginia's younger brother Jack died in a car accident. I had spent hours each day in her house doing simple tasks—folding laundry, answering the door, unloading groceries. And when I was there, I could feel the prayers for her and her family. They were as tangible as the crumb cakes and cards and flowers. Prayers for comfort and strength in the midst of the grief.

"Sometimes I feel a strange nostalgia for that week," she said. "It was so intense, and so sad, but there was something good about it, too."

"Peter said the other day that he thinks our highs will be higher and our lows will be lower than most parents'. That the joy will be more joyful, her accomplishments even more exciting. But the fear and sadness will be deeper, too."

"Yeah," she said, and she sounded like herself again, with her usual tone of thoughtful confidence. "That makes sense. And there's where I think this is different than with Jack. For us, the grief has faded, and sometimes I struggle to remember what it was about that time that was good." An image flashed into my head of Virginia, seven months pregnant, with her dad's arm around her, holding her as she wept. "I wonder whether it will be different for you. Almost like the sadness will go with you throughout Penny's life, but so will the blessing."

I hated admitting that there was grief in relation to Penny's birth, even though it was true. When Virginia called, I was feeling fine. We'd been giggling and taking pictures and were filled with the giddiness of new parents. But I didn't talk about how the grief still came, every day, and knocked me over. How we had been deeply submerged in despair last weekend, and now we were just in up to our necks. So we could breathe, could cry for help, could even get out of the water and onto dry land for a moment or two. I hadn't told her how I thought that someday we might find that the water only reached our hips and we could wade forward. And after that, merely dip a toe in now and then.

I hadn't told her how afraid I felt, afraid for the short term, that Penny wouldn't gain weight, that I wasn't feeding her enough, that my milk would dry up, that she would be too hot or too cold or too wet. And afraid for the long term: that she would die early, that she wouldn't be able to live on her own, that she wouldn't ever know deep love from one other person, a husband, that she wouldn't be able to do things she wanted to do, that her joints would be out of whack, that she wouldn't be smart or funny or cute, that other people wouldn't love her, that I wouldn't love her, that we would see her as a burden instead of a blessing.

I hadn't told her that it had to get better, the sadness, or I wouldn't survive.

Virginia waited through my silence.

I finally said, "Sorry. Lost in thought."

She said, "I'm sure you need to go, but there is one other thing I think I should tell you."

"Okay."

"When I first got your message, I was so upset. As you can tell. And I don't mean to sound all weird here, and I wasn't sure I was even going to tell you this yet, but I think I should. I was praying for you, and I was reminded of Jesus saying, 'Whoever receives this child, receives me.' So I looked it up. It's in Mark. I think I was supposed to tell you that."

Whoever receives this child.

This child.

I heard it again, that voice from the fall. *But then you wouldn't have had* this *child.*

"Thank you," I said.

I returned the phone to its receiver and stood in the hallway that stretched the length of our apartment. We had filled the wall with family photos. There was one of Mom and Dad on their wedding day, Mom reaching forward with a bright smile, Dad leaning back with his typical brooding expression. Next to them hung Peter's class photographs from kindergarten and first grade. He was easy to pick out. As an adult, his cheeks were no longer round, but he still had the dimples. Then a black-and-white photo of my great-grandparents shoulder to shoulder, with mountains in the background, in Glacier National Park. She sat up straight, in a silk suit with pearls. He looked more relaxed, with his arm slung behind her shoulder, wearing a jacket and tie. It made me smile to think of the two of them, all dressed up, exploring the wilderness. But I settled my gaze on the photographs of Peter's mother, whom we had taken to calling Grand Penny.

It had been a little over two years now since she died. And just as Virginia had said, the grief had softened. It didn't have sharp edges anymore, couldn't wake me up or interrupt my day. Her death seemed connected to this birth, in more ways than just sharing her name with her granddaughter. There was the unlikely nature of it. Grand Penny's liver cancer came out of the blue. It was simply an unpredictable menace to her body that resulted in her untimely death. Just as it was unlikely that our firstborn child would have Down syndrome. And just as out of our control.

On the face of it, these were bad things. Cancer. Down syndrome. Yet there was such grace and beauty and goodness throughout the time when Grand Penny was sick. There was even beauty in her death, amidst the horror of it all. It was a time when heaven and earth touched, when we had a glimpse of life beyond this world, of color and music and celebration. Of love.

There was something in Grand Penny's death that was linked to the birth of our daughter, that had even prepared us for her birth. Grief, yes. Grief over the loss of the baby we had expected. Grief over the difficulties and challenges she would face as she grew older. Grief over the loss of the life we thought we would lead together. But it was more than that.

At the end of Grand Penny's life, I was able to tell stories of forgiveness and healing and transformation and friendship. If that could happen in death, how much more so now, in Penny's life. It would be harder than I had ever imagined. And better, too. I had to believe that.

I looked at the pictures of Grand Penny again. There were four of them in all. Two were from her debutante year. In both, though she looked lovely, her smile seemed forced. In the third, a portrait from her days in boarding school, she gazed into the distance, her lips together. It was in the fourth picture that she stood as a mother, holding Peter on the day of his baptism. And there she smiled her smile, a smile of delight and abandon. I wished she were here to meet her granddaughter.

Mom wandered into the hallway. "Somebody's looking for you," she said.

Penny's mouth opened and closed. Time to eat.

An hour later, Peter was already fast asleep with the light on. Penny was awake, calm, looking around our bedroom. I had a rush of gratitude—for her rustling noises and Peter's breathing, his faithful presence. But even as the gratitude washed over me, the tears brimmed in my eyes. I couldn't say why exactly—fear, anger, sadness, guilt, grief? The slowly growing realization that our lives would change more than we ever could have anticipated. The constant questions I had for myself, thinking back through the months of pregnancy and the tests and the ultrasounds and the delivery itself and wondering, *What could I have done differently?* And then the countering thought that her life, extra chromosome and all, was purposeful—even, somehow, good.

Trying to make sense of it was too much. I brushed the back of my index finger against her smooth plump cheek, rocking her back and forth, lulling my own thoughts to sleep. Back and forth, back and forth, back and forth. Sleep, my child. Sleep, my child. And the reminder that came in a gentle whisper, *Whoever receives this child, receives me.*

A friend with a Down syndrome grandchild remarked upon the blessing it was to us that we didn't know ahead of time. It makes sense now that I think of it. Had I known, I would have prepared for Down syndrome. Instead, I prepared for Penny. I prepared for a child, a family, a gift—not a condition, a syndrome, a problem.

January 2006

6

Two and a half weeks into her life, we reached Penny's due date. By then Peter was not only back at work full time, but he seemed unfazed by Penny's diagnosis. After those first twenty-four hours in the hospital, he treated Down syndrome with a shrug of his shoulders, as if to say, "So what? She's our daughter. That's the important part." I wasn't there yet, but I had settled into a routine. Journaling every day. Getting outside for a walk. Nursing Penny every three hours or so, delighting in her noises as she sucked and swallowed, smiling at the milk dribbling out of her mouth as she gulped it in. I loved her soft skin against mine. I loved her features, her blue eyes watching shadows, her long eyelashes, her dimpled ears and fat cheeks. I loved being able to hold her with just one hand. I loved my love for her, a fierce, protective love that worked hard and around the clock to ward off my fears and doubts and questions.

But day after day, they found a way in. First I opened a letter from the hospital. *This letter was written to inform you that your child failed a newborn hearing screening test. Please call to schedule an appointment.*

Then the results of her blood tests came back. Just a few days after leaving the hospital, Peter and I had taken Penny back for a blood draw to confirm her diagnosis. The phlebotomist took one look at her and said, as if she were reprimanding us for our presence, "I will try once. If I don't get any blood, you'll have to bring her back when she's older." Peter held Penny, and I waited in the hallway as she screamed. But the technician had succeeded on that first try, and now I held a piece of paper that showed me Penny's chromosomal makeup in picture form. I hadn't ever seen a karyotype before, with the twenty-three pairs of chromosomes, numbers underneath. The chromosomes themselves were stumpy lines. It looked as if a child had taken a bunch of twigs and tried to pair them up on the ground. I scanned the image until I reached number 21. The twenty-first chromosomes were shorter than the others. And there they were, all in a row, like three men squatting side by side. I shook my head, not in disagreement, but with a strange sense of awe. Up until that moment, there was a part of me that thought it wasn't true. There was still a part of me that had been hoping it was all a mistake.

A few days later, a member of the local Down syndrome society called. I felt confused throughout the whole conversation, even though she was as clear and kind as she could possibly be. "I got your name from Kathy at the hospital," she explained, and I vaguely remembered one of our nurses saying she would contact a local support group for us. "I just want to welcome your daughter into the world and see if you have any questions."

On a typical day my questions looped through my brain like the words at the bottom of a CNN screen. They were constantly updated and yet always seemed to go back to the same starting point. But now that I had someone who might be able to answer them, they had disappeared. "We're doing fine," I said. "Trying to take it day by day and just figure out how we're supposed to handle all the medical stuff."

"Well, remember that no other parents were sent home from the hospital with a list of all the things that might go wrong with their baby. It sounds like Penny is doing well, so just pay attention to that. You have plenty of time to figure it out."

I started gnawing on the inside of my lip, knowing that she was probably right, but also wondering, *Shouldn't we have a therapist by now? If the first few years of brain development are the most important, aren't we missing out already?*

She interrupted my thoughts. "I also wanted to let you know that once a year, our organization has a new-parents' meeting. I know it's still early for you, but the meeting happens to be on Thursday night this week. Do you think you might want to come?"

I wrote down the information and hung up the phone. Fingering the slip of paper, I sat on our sofa for a while. Before Penny was born, Thursdays had been our date night. When we moved into the dorm, I had insisted on this weekly ritual. It was an escape from the inevitable knock on the door—a boy from the house requesting permission to go away for the weekend, a student handing in an assignment, a faculty member needing to discuss a kid in trouble. It was a refuge from the sounds of teenage boys wrestling in the corridor above our heads, from the parents who wanted to talk about their son's grade in chemistry or his failure to call home yet again this week. And it was a reason to get off campus, a reminder of us as a couple, apart from Peter's job.

The last time we had gone out to dinner was the night before Penny was born. I wanted to resume the pattern, but I hadn't expected it to start with a Down syndrome support group. The next two days, waiting for that meeting, felt like one big, deep breath of anticipation. Mom had gone home a few days earlier, but she returned to spend Thursday night. On the evening of this first outing, Penny lay in her Moses basket, gazing at a red lampshade overhead. Her Nana sat nearby, knitting a sweater for her granddaughter. She was in good hands.

When we stepped outside, the cold air felt like an affront. I squared my shoulders. Peter took my hand in his. We didn't talk in the car. We were driving through an unknown neighborhood, craning to see street signs and find the parking lot.

Our destination was the headquarters of the local Arc. I had looked it up online and I discovered that the name had originated in an acronym: The Association of Retarded Citizens. They dropped the acronym as the word *retarded* became more and more pejorative. Now it was just "the Arc." When we finally arrived, the building was dark. It took us a few tries to locate an unbolted entrance. I squeezed Peter's hand as we walked down the corridor, and a part of me was hoping that we wouldn't find the meeting after all. But I heard voices coming from a room with an open door, and soon we stood in the doorway. Ten faces turned toward us. "Hello!" and "Welcome!" and someone motioned to two empty chairs.

I had hoped it might feel like coming home, but the tone of those cheery greetings sounded false. All but three of the people around the table were relatively new parents. We all had questions. We all had fears. We all were afraid of saying the wrong thing. And there didn't seem to be anyone in charge. I had been in pastoral care classes at the seminary for two years, and I was tempted to pull out my training and ask everyone to go around the circle and share their name and where they were from and a high point and low point of their experience with their child so far. It all came out eventually, but it came in fits and starts, as if we were blindfolded—searching together, bumping into each other sometimes, groping in the dark at others. There were probably four different conversations going on at once. I caught bits and pieces.

Next to me sat Lydia. "How old is your child?" I asked.

"Three months," she said. "And you?"

"She's three weeks," I replied. "Actually, her due date was just a few days ago."

"Jayden came early, too," she said. "I guess it's pretty common."

Peter was talking with the woman next to him, Catherine. I heard her say she had gone to the University of Virginia, as had he. Her daughter Margaret was a year and a half. They had been traveling to Baltimore to visit a developmental pediatrician, but recently a local hospital had opened a clinic for kids with Down syndrome.

We shared scraps of ourselves, and the thoughts and questions started to come out. I heard about occupational therapy and physical therapy and speech delays and feeding problems. Catherine wondered out loud when she should tell her five-year-old son that his younger sister had Down syndrome. All of us with new children sat back in our chairs, our bodies speaking for us, arms crossed. The two parents of teenagers in the room leaned forward, as if they had a secret to share. They talked about their children with obvious admiration—a daughter who worked three days a week at a local mall, a son who loved art class and dancing. But I was used to stories of high school students who were reading Dickens and Shakespeare, joining the debate club, scoring a winning goal for the soccer team. And I was used to those same students, and their parents, thinking they could always work harder and achieve more. I didn't understand how art class and a minimum-wage job could even begin to compare.

Across from me sat Joe, playing games with his daughter Ella. She was the only child present, and I tried not to stare. "How big is Ella?" he said, and she threw up her arms. She caught my gaze with her bright eyes and cocked her head with an inviting smile. "She's thirteen months old, and she's not walking yet," Joe said, eyes cast down, as if he were addressing the table. "Not even crawling."

Tim, round-faced and British, replied. I could hear the pride in his voice, but I could only focus on his words, "Yes, Elizabeth isn't walking yet. Actually she's not really crawling, either."

I smiled and nodded, as if to say, *How nice*. And that's what I was thinking. *What a nice group of people. How wonderful that your little girl can smile and throw her arms in the air and that your son can write a thank-you note. How nice.* But underneath that thought and the frozen smile that accompanied it were the words, *Please, not my daughter.*

The next day I was on the phone with an old friend. She had four kids, and the youngest had been born just a few months before Penny. When I asked her, "How are things in your household?" she talked about being tired of nursing already and how the fourth time around it was easier to know what to do and harder to keep her household in order. I was refreshed by her candor, by the ordinary banter, and then she said, "Of course, it would help if my husband could get his act together. The other day, I fished another beer can out of the trash. It's like he just can't remember that we recycle. I mean what is he, retarded?"

My heart started pounding so hard that I didn't hear the rest of the thought. I tried to force a short laugh, to pretend that it was nothing. She didn't seem to notice the change.

After I hung up the phone, I sat with Penny. I leaned against the cushions, her head upon my knees, her body supported by my legs. I gazed at her—black hair and fat cheeks and crinkly ears and pink lips and ever-so-slightly upturned eyes. She was so cuddly and lively. She sat on my lap and wiggled her fingers and cooed. And already, she worked so hard. The night before, Peter had placed her facedown on the floor with his hands behind her feet, and, to a chorus of encouragement, she had pushed against his palms with a series of grunts and cries. She spent hours every day gazing at patterns and the face of any new person who stopped by. I still couldn't believe those words that first had been uttered in the hospital and that showed up whenever I read information about Down syndrome: *mental retardation.* I couldn't believe she would be slowed down, delayed. But that was our new reality, wasn't it?

I thought back to the phone conversation, to the answer I hadn't given my friend. *No, your husband, who went to an*

Ivy League school and has a master's degree, is not retarded. But my daughter is.

Every visitor seemed to bring with them a reminder of the distance. One day I mentioned that Penny had gained nine ounces, and one of Peter's colleagues said with a smile, "Life. It's all about cell division, cell division, cell division." She had no reason to think that her words would fall like a blow. But for Penny, as each cell replicated itself, it passed along extra, abnormal genetic material. I feared Penny would, with time, be overtaken by that extra chromosome. That she would become less and less herself, more and more defined by her diagnosis.

At least once a day someone told me, "Down's babies are so cute," and I wondered if they could see Penny when they looked at her, or if they could only see her diagnosis—the pudgy face and tiny features and the extra fold of skin around the eyes. It felt as though everything came back to Down syndrome. "Down syndrome babies are so pleasant," or "She will be stubborn . . . happy . . . an angel . . ." No one made such blanket predictions about other babies. It was as if instead of giving her credit for being delightful, Down syndrome got the credit. The extra chromosome got the credit.

And then there was the long line of people who wanted to insist that our situation wasn't any different from most parents'. I would smile and nod when they said, "None of us can predict what will happen with our children." I wanted to explain that part of what they were saying was true—none of us can predict whether our kids will break the law or fail a test or get mono, and it was no less likely that Penny would get hit by a car than Emma or Peyton or Hallie or Maddie. I wanted to pull out the lists and charts that said Penny would certainly need physical therapy, had a 75 percent chance of hearing loss, and a higher likelihood of childhood leukemia. I wanted to ask them if they had gotten an email recently about becoming the legal guardian of their child when he or she reached eighteen years of age. Sure, none of us could predict the bad stuff. But I was walking around with guarantees of it. Guarantees that this little girl—whose cries calmed when I walked into the room, whose soft body nuzzled against my chest, whose delicate fingers curled around mine, whose eyes seemed to drink in the features of my face—that this delightful daughter of mine was going to endure a list of things that I would never choose for her.

A part of me wanted to run back to the Arc and reconvene that group of parents, to run away from all the generalizations and comparisons and careless comments, to declare that they were not only my new friends but my only friends, the only ones who could possibly understand. Instead, I found myself giving people permission to talk about Down syndrome. Even people who knew us well seemed to need me to bring it up, or else it became taboo—the topic on everyone's mind without ever being broached.

And in the midst of all the visitors, all the information, all the frustration and words I wished hadn't been said, I received an email from an old friend. It said, "I can't wait to see the ministry that Penny will have." It hadn't crossed my mind that Penny would have a "ministry," a means of giving to other people. And that simple sentence, with its hopeful words, made me realize that as much as I insisted that our experience was different from other parents', and that our child was different from other children, *different* didn't mean *less than*. Penny would give to us. She would not only be blessed. She would be a blessing.

I went to the doctor for a follow-up appointment today. The receptionist was very nice. She told me about a good friend of hers who has a daughter with Down syndrome. The young woman is in her mid-20s, with a job, with highlights in her hair. I think the receptionist was trying to comfort me by giving an example of how functional someone with Down syndrome can be, but her words betrayed her. She said things like, "They dress her in cute, funky clothes," and, "She can walk around the neighborhood all by herself and the neighbors keep an eye on her." What I heard was not that she wears cute clothes and goes for walks, but that her mom still chooses those clothes, she can't drive, and she needs the neighbors to look out for her on a walk around the block. I didn't feel particularly consoled.

People are always trying to downplay the hard part and overemphasize the good instead of letting the tension remain.

February 2006

7

There were days when I woke up and felt like any other new parent. I kept a daily log, recording how long Penny nursed on each side, how often she urinated, when we gave her a bath. We bumbled our way through her one-month checkup. I somehow managed to bring a diaper bag with no extra diaper, leaving the pediatrician to construct one for us out of plastic "hazardous waste" bags, paper towels, and Band-Aids. One day Peter found me at eleven in the morning in my pajamas, in tears because we had run out of bananas.

We made mistakes. We felt overwhelmed. And we recorded all the ordinary details of life that had suddenly taken on new meaning because they were hers for the first time. There was the record of Penny's first snowfall, her first walk outside, her first bottle with her dad, the first time we caught her smiling in her sleep.

And then there was her first overnight alone with me. In the middle of February, Peter headed north to coach the girls' varsity squash team in the National Championships. I felt a pang of longing as he said good-bye, with a kiss on Penny's forehead and a longer kiss on the lips for me. Stuck in my throat were the words "Don't go." But he had an obligation to the team, and he enjoyed coaching, and I would be fine at home, just fine.

Peter grew up loving sports. Skiing, kayaking, tennis, soccer, baseball, golf, gymnastics, riding his bike around the neighborhood—he had stories to go along with just about any physical activity imaginable. He spent much of his childhood in New Orleans, so squash had been a new challenge for him when he arrived at a Connecticut boarding school in ninth grade. He picked up a racquet and learned to play, adjusting to the game's geometry, bouncing the hard black ball off all four walls, training his body to swing from high to low and take long strides rather than short steps. His team had made it to the finals of the New England Championships his senior year. Ten years later, he could still give me a point-by-point description of the tournament.

I had never been much of an athlete. I spent my early years in a small town in North Carolina where piano lessons and ballet classes took up our afternoons. By the time my dad's job prompted a move to Connecticut, I had decided it was too late for me to pick up sports. In high school, when an afternoon activity was required, I had shown up for soccer practice in Keds. I hadn't owned running shoes or cleats.

I had trouble understanding Peter's love for physical activity and his competitive spirit, but I knew that getting himself out to the courts every day, exhorting those girls to play better and work harder, really mattered to him. When Penny was born, a colleague had offered to take over his coaching responsibilities. But he didn't want the help. He had gone to practice two days after we came home from the hospital, and he told the girls the whole story about Penny. As he walked out the door for the tournament, I managed to say, "Have a great weekend. I hope the girls play really well."

It started to snow the next day. Big light flakes spinning their way to the ground. A quiet blanket of white, outlining the limbs of the trees and the rooflines, covering the paths and roads and cars. I sat in the front room of our apartment with Penny nestled against my body, rocking back and forth, gazing at the snow.

Before long, I turned my gaze to the child in my arms, hearing Peter's words from a few nights before: "It is so hard to believe you are going to face the challenges you are going to face."

Her big blue eyes were locked on mine, studying me. I thought back to her bath, her array of facial expressions, her baby smell. The way she grasped my hand with her warm little fingers and held on. The way she tracked objects with her eyes and calmed herself to sleep. Her hands discovering her mouth. It all seemed so normal. So hard to believe.

When I awoke in the middle of the night to nurse Penny, the snow continued to fall. All through the next day, it snowed. Peter and his team were stranded three hours away.

We talked a few times each day. I reported on Penny's naps, on the hour she spent lying on my chest, her feeding schedule. I heard the squash scores. We compared notes on the weather. Eight inches on the ground in New Jersey. Two feet in Connecticut, but now the sun was shining.

On Sunday night when he called, his voice sounded different. It wasn't the clipped tone of a reporter. It was the voice I had fallen in love with, the voice that had told me the story of his grandfather's death, the voice he used when he couldn't figure out what to do, the voice that came out whenever he shared memories of laughing with his mom.

"I was crossing the street with the team," he said. "There's just so much snow. It's hard to even describe it. And on the sides of the road there's even more from the plows. Anyway, we were crossing the street and I turned around for some reason. It was really sunny, but something caught my eye. There was a woman in a puffy red parka. She was struggling to get through a snowbank. So I told the team to go ahead, and I went back to help her. I took her hand. She was all bundled up, so I just glimpsed her face. It was only as I watched her walk away that I realized she had Down syndrome." He paused. Almost in a whisper, he said, "I just hope there will be someone who goes out of their way to help our daughter cross the street."

"I wish you were here," I said. "I love you."

After we hung up the phone, I relived his story in my mind. I could see it—the sunlight glinting off the snow, Peter in his navy blue corduroys and boots rushing to her aid, the look of relief on the woman's face. I could feel it, too—the kindness he offered before he even knew what he was offering. But I couldn't imagine how she would have felt. Had it become commonplace to need help? Was it frustrating? Did she want to resist his hand and do it herself?

From the outside, anyone who looked in on my life would have said I had never needed much help. The same was true for Peter. We had always been able to do it alone. But now people looked at me and they saw my daughter. Just a few days earlier, a friend had said, "I can see Penny's Down's because of her mouth and tongue." It was an innocuous comment, but with it I realized how quickly people would judge her based upon her appearance. And many of those judgments would be negative ones or at least fearful, ignorant ones. I then realized that when anyone saw me or Peter, they usually had immediate positive impressions—well-dressed, good looking, in-shape. Acceptable. But now we were bound to our daughter—our beautiful, cuddly, disabled daughter—and so her vulnerability, her weaknesses, her needs had become our own.

About a year into our marriage, Peter and I had been eating dinner and one of us said, "Have you ever thought about never having kids?" and the other replied, "Yes!" When we referred to the conversation later, we couldn't even remember who brought it up, since both of us had been thinking it for so long. We had been the first of our friends to get married, but as other peers started bearing children, we realized we weren't so sure. There were plenty of reasons for our ambivalence. Peter's parents had divorced when he was young. We worked with high school students and felt as though we had plenty of time with kids as it was. We liked each other's company and had no sense that there was something missing. But really, it came down to limitations. We liked having the freedom—the finances, the time—to travel to Europe once a year. We liked sleeping in on the weekends. We liked long road trips and working late and controlling our schedules.

And here we were, with a child who would limit us more than we had ever imagined. Penny would walk later than other kids and with less stability. Her body was more prone to infection. She would have trouble solving problems. She might never live on her own.

When I was pregnant, a woman had said to me, "When you have a child, you find that your heart is beating in someone else's body."

Her words had struck me as an exaggeration, and a somewhat dramatic one at that. But I was starting to understand what she meant. Nearly every day I bumped into an assumption about who Penny was supposed to be, and every time it felt as though I reopened a wound. Months earlier, I wouldn't have paused when I read in a baby book about "the perfect 46 chromosomes" that make up your child. I wouldn't have noticed when the woman who cut my hair said, "You've got to have your kids young, before you're thirty-five, you know, so they won't be screwed up." I wouldn't have gulped at the reference in the *Time* article to the "seemingly hopeless diagnosis of mental retardation." I wouldn't have thrown away the *Parents* magazine with the cover that asked, "Will your child be tall? Athletic? Intelligent?" And I wouldn't have wondered whether all those assumptions might have been wrong.

Peter returned from New Haven on Monday night, after five days away. Penny was asleep, swaddled in a pink-and-white striped blanket, and I was already in bed. He scooped her up from her Moses basket and climbed in next to me.

"If you could take away the extra chromosome," I asked, "would you?"

He took a long time to respond. I kept my eyes fixed on the smooth skin of Penny's face. I swelled with pride just thinking about the way she had lifted her head while lying on my chest earlier in the day. And then Peter said softly, "Yes. If I could take it away, I would."

I nodded. So would I.

I knew it was an impossible exercise, to consider extracting that genetic material from every cell in her body, to think of changing her molecular structure altogether. I knew it was an impossible question, an admission of helplessness even to ask it. And Jesus's words returned: "Whoever receives this child, receives me."

Those words haunted me. I didn't open my Bible often those days. I didn't pray much, either. I would have liked to ignore God altogether, but my whole adult life had been consumed with Christianity. I couldn't get away, even though a part of me wanted to. We had been studying John's gospel in church that fall, and I couldn't stop thinking about the very last chapter, where Jesus told Peter that when he got older, "Someone will dress you and lead you where you do not want to go." And then Jesus said, "Follow me!"

The words came as a message across the years, although I wasn't sure whether to take them as a command or an invitation. *Follow me where you do not want to go.*

I looked up the passage. It occurred after Jesus' resurrection, when the disciples were unsure of themselves, unsure what had happened to their leader, unsure whether they might be the next ones to die. So they went fishing. They went back to what they knew how to do. They went back to a familiar place. It didn't go well. They didn't catch anything until a man showed up on the beach and told them to throw their nets in one more time. And then they hauled in an abundance. Luke told a similar story, but his version showed up much earlier in Jesus' ministry, when Jesus first called the disciples. I knew that some scholars saw this passage from John as a retelling of the same scene, but I saw it as Jesus's way of saying, "Don't you remember how I called you the first time? I know it's been rough lately, but this life with me is about abundance. Don't you remember?"

I closed the Bible, my finger holding my place. There was so much of me that didn't want to remember the abundance of my life as a Christian. I had a shelf of journals, and I could take down any one of them to find answered prayers, verses from the Bible that spoke to my everyday life, whispers from the Spirit of comfort, purpose, blessing. And here was Jesus saying, "Don't you remember?"

I couldn't forget. The time on the beach where I had heard words as distinct as an audible voice saying, "I am with you." The time I met Peter, certain that God had brought us together. The time in college when I was afraid to go back to school and said to my mother, "I just want someone to be there with me and hold my hand." That same evening I had gone upstairs and picked up a dusty book filled with Bible verses from the bottom shelf of my bedside table. I opened at random and read, "For I am the Lord your God who takes hold of your right hand and says to you, 'Do not fear; I will help you.'" And when I returned to school the next day, there was a card from my grandmother in my mailbox. Printed on the inside was the same verse, as if God had wanted to make sure I was paying attention.

The stories continued. They took me all the way to that moment in the car, seven months pregnant, when I heard the words, *But then you wouldn't have had* this *child*. And again, yes. This child is the one I want. This child is the one I need.

Even now, if I wanted to tell a story about God's provision, I could. I felt alone, but there was the Down syndrome support group with five or six other young couples who lived within a ten-mile radius of our home. The president of the group had told us that in her twenty-year history with the organization, there had never been so many parents with kids so close in age. We decided to start a monthly Friday morning gathering of mothers and children, with no agenda other than getting to know each other. I had been given this group of people, even though a part of me wanted to resist the gift.

I reopened the Bible and continued reading. Jesus had cooked breakfast for the disciples on the beach. I loved how mundane it was. Every example I had of God's "miraculous" provision in my life was a lot like this one. No one could ever prove that Jesus had put those fish in the water. The miracle wasn't a display of power. It was a reminder of who He was—the one who cared for them with abundance. The one who served them. It was a reminder of who they were—the ones called to receive from Him. The ones called to follow Him.

And as they were eating breakfast, Jesus turned to Peter. Three times, He asked Peter if he loved Him. Three times, Peter said yes. He reversed the three denials he had uttered as Jesus went to His death. And then Jesus commissioned Peter to "feed His sheep." It all seemed so lovely up to this point: Jesus performed miracles, cooked breakfast, forgave Peter, and sent him out with renewed purpose. But then I remembered that Jesus was always telling His disciples that following Him involved suffering.

It seemed silly to think of the birth of our daughter as a form of suffering. Jesus talked about the suffering of being whipped and scorned and executed. How could the birth of a child with Down syndrome compare to a martyr's death? And yet every time I recognized the purity of my love for Penny, I was dying to an old part of myself, an old part that thought the only ones worth loving were the ones who could be productive and articulate and considered attractive and successful.

Over the course of Penny's short time with us, Peter and I had already talked about what her future might look like. "Do you think she'll be able to have a job?" I asked.

"Someone told me about their friend's brother who has Down syndrome and washes dishes." He looked up quickly and said, "Not that she'll wash dishes . . ."

But maybe our daughter would grow up to wash dishes. Maybe she would be able to serve joyfully in what to us would be a lifeless job. I had heard it before—"If you're a street cleaner, clean to the glory of God." And I had never understood that sentiment. But I could imagine Penny doing exactly that. And I could imagine being proud of her for it.

Jesus reminded His friend Peter of their history together. He cooked Peter breakfast. He forgave him. He gave him a purpose. And then He told him that he would suffer. But reading back over those words, I noticed that Jesus didn't ask Peter to embrace his suffering. He was honest that Peter would be taken where he did not want to go. There was no sentimentality. No false piety. No stoicism. Just a statement of reality: The road ahead would be hard, but this is the road where I will be with you.

Follow me where you do not want to go.

Penny would have Down syndrome no matter what. The call to me was to follow Jesus down that road rather than trying to navigate it on my own. And to trust that the rocky parts would be smoother with Him as a guide, and that the scenery would even be beautiful much of the time.

That first night when Peter was home from the tournament, I asked him to tell me about the woman with the puffy red parka one more time. His story held the vulnerability, the exposure, the hurt, alongside the joy of human connection, of giving and receiving. Before we went to bed, he said it again, "I just hope someone will go out of their way to help our daughter across the street."

Penny is lying in the middle of our bed, staring at a small stuffed panda. She is enamored—her eyes light up and she bats with her hand to touch him and she almost smiles. Her hair has grown over her ears. It sticks up in front as though she were a high school boy who just discovered the wonders of gel. She is so bright and beautiful, and as I think about the fact (not likelihood, not prediction—the fact, the reality) that her development will slow down from here, I feel like we will be losing her, that she will always be fading away rather than coming to life. . . .

February 2006

8

March brought with it harbingers of spring—a few more minutes of daylight, a hint of warmth underneath the chill, crocuses poking their purple and white heads out of the ground. And like those flowers, with their tentative but persistent movement toward the sun, I started to venture forth with Penny.

First I reported back to the hospital for another hearing test. I was greeted by a petite woman with long black hair. I never learned her name or title. She scowled for a moment upon viewing us. "Come this way."

She led me to the delivery floor, past the nurse's station, past the reminders of Penny's entrance into the world, the memory of that speck of blood on Peter's shirt, those moments I had replayed in my brain for the past two months as if somehow I could rewind the tape and change the story. She led me into a dimly lit room filled with unused equipment. I wondered if this had been where the doctors had told Peter the news.

"The test will take about an hour," she said. "You'll need to keep her asleep."

"I'll do my best," I replied, trying to mask my disbelief. I swaddled Penny and gave her a pacifier and started bouncing. Within moments, she had fallen asleep. The woman placed probes on Penny's head and in her ears. I pulled a plastic chair next to the machine and sat in silence, rocking Penny any time she stirred. An hour later, the woman said, "She has a mild to moderate hearing loss in both ears."

"Is it permanent?" I asked.

"Probably not. The findings are consistent with fluid buildup. It could even be amniotic fluid that remained after birth. It may clear up with time. It may not."

"If it doesn't, then what do we do?"

"You can try tubes in her ears, although we can't be sure that will fix the problem. She may always have this level of hearing loss, which means she'll have trouble with certain frequencies and with sounds like *sh* and *th*."

I nodded. My demeanor didn't change, even though inside I was shouting: *Have you noticed that this is my child we're talking about?* I stood up, and Penny opened her eyes. I kissed her on the forehead. *Do you know what it feels like to sing to your baby and wonder if she can hear you?* I didn't want any more medical information. I didn't want any more news about what might slow Penny down or the therapies she might need or the problems she might encounter. All I wanted was to get out of the room.

But the woman said, "You should see an otolaryngologist."

"Excuse me?"

"An otolaryngologist. An ENT. Ear, nose, and throat doctor. They might want to schedule a surgery soon."

I shouldered the diaper bag. "Okay. Will do."

Peter took the news with more levity. When I mentioned the sounds Penny would have trouble hearing, he said, "Good thing we didn't name her Sheila."

As the list of medical tests and evaluations grew, my new friends with children with Down syndrome directed me toward the Children's Hospital of Philadelphia, which they all referred to as CHOP. I made one appointment for an ultrasound of Penny's hips (her pediatrician said they were so loose they might be out of their sockets) and another for an ultrasound of her brain (to check on an abnormality picked up in utero). Next on the list were the otolaryngologist and a visit to a genetic counselor. I started with the ENT.

After requesting the customary information—name, date of birth—the receptionist asked, "And what is the nature of your visit?"

"Well, she was born with Down syndrome and she failed her newborn hearing test. And then a follow-up test suggested that she has a mild to moderate hearing loss in both ears and the person who did the test said we needed to see a doctor."

"Oh my," she said.

Even though she couldn't see me, I felt my eyes blinking rapidly, as if I could communicate my confusion over her response. Before I said anything else, she asked, "Did you know? Ahead of time, I mean. Did you know?"

"About the Down syndrome?" Of course she meant the Down syndrome. "No, we didn't know ahead of time."

"Oh my," she said again.

"Yes, well, I'm just calling to see when I can get an appointment."

"Right. Okay." She paused, and I envisioned her frowning at a computer screen. "No," she said, "that's too long. I'll tell you what. I'm going to put you in next week."

"But I thought there would be a wait . . ."

"I think it's important that your daughter see a doctor," she replied.

"Well. Thank you."

The next call brought more of the same. The receptionist at the genetic counseling department insisted that I speak directly to a nurse practitioner, and then they agreed we shouldn't wait for the next available appointment. The doctor would see us in ten days.

I hung up the phone and looked around our living room. I couldn't quite figure out why we, among all the patients at CHOP, warranted the special treatment. It was as if I had shown up at the end of a long line and everyone insisted I move directly to the front with the words, "Yours really is the exceptional case. This is a VERY BIG DEAL. We rearrange our plans for situations like yours."

I couldn't decide if I agreed. Sure, Penny had an extra chromosome in every cell of her body. That was a big deal. And every week brought news of another specialist we'd need to see someday. And yet she also seemed so much like any other baby, except easier, actually. She had started sleeping ten hours a night without any coaxing. And when she awoke, around six thirty, she was often content to lie in her crib for ten or fifteen minutes just cooing and looking around until I had roused myself enough to attend to her. Her eyes lit up when she saw Peter or me. She cuddled and cried and ate and slept. What was so different? What was so exceptional? What was so wrong?

I soon discovered some of the pediatrician's fears were unfounded. Penny's hips were fine. The brain ultrasound showed a "normal variant" that probably wouldn't pose a problem. Missy, Penny's therapist, showed up for her first visit and told us she was doing "great." We had a scare when Dr. Bill detected a heart murmur, followed by a visit to the cardiologist who discovered Penny had an open blood vessel between her heart and her lungs. But even there, the doctors didn't register grave concern. If it didn't close on its own, they would perform a simple surgical procedure when she was older. So the books and charts, the response of the receptionists, the terrifying statistics—they didn't line up with what I was experiencing in our little girl.

My mother came to spend the night every Thursday. She drove the two hours south to visit her granddaughter, but she also came for me. As the oldest of four, I had always been independent and responsible. When I was a kid, I unloaded the dishwasher without needing to be asked. I wrote down phone messages. I never broke the rules. At age thirteen, I had gone away to school. I saw my family every couple of weeks and talked to my parents on the phone every Sunday. I had done much of my growing up on my own.

And yet, when Penny arrived, I needed my mom. I needed someone to teach me lullabies, to reassure me it was okay to let a baby cry, someone to help fold the laundry and listen to my fears and tell me to go take a nap. But I also needed the comfort of the woman who loved me like I loved Penny, the woman whose love meant she would give all she could to care for me, to keep me safe.

That week when Mom arrived, we bundled Penny into the stroller and headed outside. Penny lay on her back with a cotton hat that looked like a strawberry perched on her head and a blanket to protect her body against the breeze. Her eyes darted around—watching the bare branches as we walked under an oak tree, shifting her gaze to me, then studying her hands.

"What are you reading these days?" I asked Mom.

"Oh, a book for book club," she replied. "*March*. It's written from the perspective of the father in *Little Women*."

I could feel my throat tightening. I wondered why I had even asked the question. It was one of the things I couldn't stop thinking about, that Penny wouldn't share my love for books, for words, for reading and writing. That I'd never be able to give this part of myself to my daughter.

"Mom," I said, "Penny's so alert and so sweet right now, but sometimes I'm afraid she'll seem less and less alive the more she grows up. Everything I read says that she'll start slowing down, physically and mentally, and I feel like we'll start losing her then."

Mom took a minute to reply. Her hair was pulled back into a ponytail, showing her earrings, two cat's eyes. Every week it was a different pair, each chosen for the enjoyment of her preschool class. Her face had a few lines on it, but she still looked young to me, young and strong. She said, "Just because *you* come alive through the intellect, and just because Penny won't share that with you, doesn't mean that she won't come alive. She will come alive. It will just be in ways that are different from you." She kept her eyes on Penny as she spoke, and her voice held a measure of wonder.

"You know," Mom said, "you're the only one of my daughters who talks to me about books."

Kate had never been a reader. She ran a dance studio, and she and Mom shared a love of teaching young children. Brooks connected with Mom through sewing and painting. Elly had a newfound interest in cooking and gardening. But beyond those points of connection, Mom had always been available to listen to us—in car rides from one activity to another, in the kitchen as we complained about school or boys or friendships while she cooked dinner, even late at night when we woke her up to tell her we had come home. It was her presence that made a difference, not shared interests. I only hoped I could give the same to Penny.

When we got back to the apartment, Mom, in her gentle but firm way, sent me to my room. "Take some time for yourself" was all she said.

I picked up my journal and climbed into bed, still thinking about our conversation, trying to puzzle through the intense sadness that gripped me every time I thought about Penny and reading. I considered the words used to describe intelligence. Terms associated with light and precision: bright, brilliant, sharp, smart. Their converse: dull, faded, drab. But Penny's eyes were full of light and her face and body full of life and movement. I pictured her delight when she found her mouth with her fingers, her look of astonishment after a burp, the stern concentration on her face as she prepared to swat at a toy.

Up until then, every time I thought about having a daughter with mental retardation, I had thought about it in the ways it would be beneficial for me. I knew my love for Penny was shattering idols and overturning prejudices and teaching me to value so much more beyond the life of the mind. But as I lay in my bedroom trying to put my thoughts on paper, I finally admitted just how important words were to me, how much a part of my life, how integral they were to who I was and to what made me happy and to how I loved and served others. I let the tears come, grieving the thought that there was a part of me my daughter would never know.

But after that day, whenever the same sadness arose, it led me back to the questions Mom had provoked. What, if anything, was there to be sad about? Was every life meant to include a certain IQ score, physical prowess, perfect sight and hearing?

I realized that I had always assumed it was very sad to have a child with mental retardation, or, for that matter, to be a person with mental retardation. But why? Why was that sad—because our culture held the intellect in such high regard? Because life was only as valuable as what we could produce or what academic degrees we had attained or how attractive we were or how big our house was? What was sad about having a child with Down syndrome?

I started going for a walk with Penny every day. The green shoots of daffodils strained toward the sky. The trees grew buds and the earth absorbed the morning dew. And I finally realized that my real question had to do with goodness—what, if anything, in how Penny had been formed was not good? In a Nietzchean universe, of course, her existence was a tragedy, plain and simple—an accident, an abnormality, biology "gone wrong." But in a God-created universe, what was good and not good in her? And was it any different from that which was good and not good in the rest of us?

As we walked, I narrated our surroundings. I pointed out the pond, the geese, the ducks, and even a blue heron. It struck me that it was not good that Penny had fluid in her ears that impeded her ability to hear. Something good could come of it, of course, but in and of itself it was not good for her to be cut off from a form of communication and interaction with others. I thought about our friend whose daughter had autism and the way her parents described her alienation from the rest of the family, even from herself. My friend's daughter was a human being with gifts to offer. And yet it was not good for her to be separated from relationships with her family. Or I thought about my friend whose daughter was diagnosed with anencephaly in utero. The doctors had all assumed she would abort the baby, but she insisted on carrying her to term. "My daughter is alive until she dies," my friend had said. She had recognized the value in her daughter's life, but it was not good that her life was cut short.

I still wondered, was mental retardation inherently not good? Or did it just seem not good because it was not something that I wanted or knew how to understand?

My thoughts went back to the idea of the kingdom of God. Between Jesus's parables and the biblical descriptions of the new heavens and the new earth, I had a picture in my mind of what life would be like without sin, without separation, without everything that is not good. Would Penny be herself in these new heavens and new earth? Would I recognize her? Or would that extra chromosome be taken away, altering her appearance and her intelligence and her capabilities and her personality?

I thought about Jesus, with the marks of His suffering on the cross still inscribed upon His hands and side even after the resurrection. And it seemed to me we would bear our wounds in heaven—we would look the same and very different all at once. It made me think Penny would both look like herself and be transformed. As would I.

After weeks of thinking about Penny and about what was not good in her, I finally realized that there was just as much—no, there was more—that was not good in me. All the pettiness, all the judgment, all the bias. Over and over again, I had thought about who she might have been if that extra chromosome hadn't gotten stuck in that first moment of conception. I couldn't escape wondering about the "real" Penny, my daughter who seemed hidden behind her diagnosis. I had wanted to be able to change her instead of receiving change myself.

Penny and I might never talk about literature together. But I had to trust that we would continue to communicate love to each other. That the way she nestled against my chest and calmed under my touch would one day translate into words that said the same. And I had to trust that she would keep growing up and become even more who she was: bright, delightful, a joy. I had to trust that I, too, would keep growing up. It wasn't hard to believe that love would keep changing me.

I remember arriving by train in Prague last summer. The station was dirty, the language unfamiliar, we couldn't speak or read the alphabet, and we had no currency. Our first cab ride was a rip-off. The driver overcharged the ignorant Americans. I remember feeling—in spite of all the wonderful things I had heard and read about Prague—that I wanted to go home. I wanted to go home where it was familiar and predictable and safe.

I have had this same feeling since Penny was born. I am told that life with a child with Down syndrome will be full of grace—blessings abundant, joy, beauty. But often it is simply overwhelming, foreign, scary, and I no longer want the adventure. I want to forgo the benefits in light of the discomfort and unknowns. Yes, that is what I often feel. I want to go home.

February 2006

9

"I miss my wife."

He said it softly, almost under his breath. A lone tear made its way down his cheek.

"I hate to say it, but I feel like I'm competing with our daughter."

I leaned against Peter's shoulder and took his hand, grateful for the familiar warmth of his body behind mine. I hadn't expected his words, and yet as they lingered in the room, heavy with months of waiting to be spoken aloud, I understood. It had been just the two of us for so long. We had met in high school—he the handsome troublemaker who went from one girlfriend to the next, me the bookish girl who never went to parties. I could still remember our first conversation, standing in darkness, talking about friendship. He had surprised me then with his thoughtfulness and his honesty. He had surprised me even more when he initiated another conversation, and another, and another. Within ten days we were an official couple, through the rest of high school and college. We married three weeks after his graduation. Now, nearly seven years from our wedding day, he was still my best friend.

Silence covered us. I listened to him breathing, felt the slight shudder in his chest from the tears, ran my thumb over his knuckles, placed my fingers inside the palm of this hand I knew so well. And for a while all I did was think about our years together. The time we took a walk through the leaves on a cool day that first fall when we were dating. Or the time he packed a picnic on the beach and refused to break up with me even though I deserved it. Or the night we stayed up past midnight painting our bedroom a green the color of a Granny Smith apple, which we regretted in the light of day. His first visit to my parents' house, when he danced with my little sisters in the attic. The times he held my hand and listened as I panicked about a paper I had to write. The night he proposed, in the same spot where we had met as teenagers.

And I thought about our years at Lawrenceville. Even though I hadn't been employed by the school, we always had seen ourselves as a team. We invited his students over for meals. I knew the boys who lived in our house, and I generally sat downstairs with them for a while on Saturday nights when Peter was on duty. I knew what topics he was teaching and whether his kids' writing was getting any better. I helped him plan his syllabi. I even checked his email for him when he couldn't keep up. But for the past few months, from the end of the pregnancy through the beginning of Penny's life, I hadn't heard much at all about his work. I hadn't asked about his students, what he was teaching, what he was thinking when it came to the classroom or the squash courts or the boys in the house. I certainly hadn't asked how I could help.

"I'm sorry," I finally said.

"I feel selfish even bringing it up. You're here all day, and you do everything for her. I just come in and make faces for a few minutes." He rested his chin on the top of my head.

"I remember something you said when I was pregnant. You said that having a child would give us more of each other. That I'd get to see you as a dad and you'd get to see me as a mom. This was supposed to bring us together. But I don't blame you for feeling abandoned. I didn't realize . . . I'm sorry."

Our days were so different now. He put on a coat and tie every morning, ate his cereal and drank his coffee, kissed us good-bye, and walked out the door. He went on to interact with hundreds of people—lunch with colleagues, meetings about students in trouble, teaching, coaching. He came home in the evening, helped bathe Penny and put her to sleep, and we ate dinner together. Those dinner conversations were almost always a record of my day—the phone calls I'd made to doctors, the visits from therapists, the reading I'd done. My thoughts were consumed by our daughter.

I would report what I was learning: "Did you know the average age a kid with Down syndrome learns to ride a bike is ten?" Or I'd give him a detailed rundown of our schedule, when she slept and how much she ate. There were times he found me on the verge of tears—feeling fat and incompetent and worried I would never be interested in anything outside our home again. And days he found me beaming, hoping Penny would reproduce for him whatever feat I had seen that afternoon—grabbing a toy with two hands, smiling at me, turning her head from left to right.

It didn't help that we had responded to Penny's diagnosis so differently. Two days after our return from the hospital, Peter finished grieving and walked outside and never looked back. Penny was his beautiful daughter, and that was that. I trusted him—he had immersed himself in grief and had emerged ready to receive our daughter. He didn't worry about her future. He didn't wrestle with the theological questions surrounding Down syndrome. He just loved her.

I wasn't there yet. I felt too fragile. Too protective of Penny. Too worried that I would hear comments or catch people staring. He didn't push me. We knew from past experience that we would each work things out in time. So it wasn't judgment that divided us. It was just difference.

We still spent time alone together. Every Thursday night, after Penny went to bed and with my mom as our baby-sitter, we went out to dinner. I always felt like an imposter—dressed up and eating a nice meal, and our daughter had Down syndrome. It was as if I thought that a prerequisite for eating pear and goat cheese salad was an absence of life's complications. As if I thought that all the other people in the restaurant lived lives of ease. I guess part of it was that a date with my husband felt so familiar, eerily familiar, so disconnected from this new life I lived as a mother, this new life I lived as a mother of a child with special needs.

But even on the nights alone together, Down syndrome was all I could talk about. One of those evenings, I looked up from my salad and asked, "Do you blame me?"

Peter squinted a little, the way he did when he was confused. "Blame you for what?"

I felt a catch in my throat. "For the Down syndrome. For the extra chromosome. I read that it usually comes from the mother."

He put his fork down and reached out his hand. "It hasn't crossed my mind. No."

I rested my hand in his, but I continued, "Because I really think it might be my fault. Because you know, usually it happens with older women. It made me think—what if my eggs, even though I'm only twenty-eight, what if my eggs are old? And what if that's because I had an eating disorder? I've always heard that eating disorders can mess up fertility. What if I did this?" I blinked and looked away.

"Age," he said, his voice low and gentle. "You didn't do this. God did this. Penny is our daughter. That's all that matters. There's no one to blame. You aren't allowed to take responsibility."

The catch in my throat started to soften.

He squeezed my hand and picked up his fork.

"One more thing?" I asked.

Peter nodded.

"I've also been thinking that most babies with Down syndrome don't make it. Even the ones who aren't aborted, often their lives end in miscarriage. From what I've read, it's something like 75 percent. So I thought if I'm going to feel guilty that she has an extra chromosome, then at least I can also feel proud that my body carried her to term."

He shook his head. "Or you can just be grateful that she's healthy and you're healthy and we've got a wonderful family."

The waiter cleared our plates and I laid my hands on the white tablecloth. I kept my eyes down, studying the ring on my right hand, a gift from my grandmother for my twenty-first birthday. Then I gazed at the diamond on my left hand that had come from Peter two days later, when he proposed.

"It's funny," I said. "For all those years that I didn't think we'd have kids, once we decided to get pregnant, I always expected a big family."

Peter sat back in his chair. "But?"

"Well, I don't know how to think about having more kids now."

After Penny was born, the doctors told us it had been "random" for me to conceive a child with Down syndrome. And I thought "random" meant it could never happen again, or at least that I went back into the same statistical pool as all the other twenty-eight-year-old women, with a 1 in 1,000 chance of having a child with Down syndrome. But then we had learned that my chance of having another was 1 in 100, as if my womb had just catapulted forward a decade.

"It makes me mad at the doctors, really," I said. I could hear the indignation in my voice. I pictured the entire medical establishment as a middle-aged man with a slight paunch and a smug expression. I wanted to force that man to admit that there were some things he just didn't know. I wanted him to uncross his arms and lose the smile and feel helpless. I wanted to punch him in the stomach and watch his eyes get big. "When they say that Down syndrome is random, they're basically lying. What they mean is that they don't know why it happened. That's all." I took a breath. "Sorry."

"Are you done?" Peter asked. He held my gaze with kindness in his eyes, as if he would gladly listen to anything I needed to say.

"I'm done. But I'm still wondering what you think about having other kids."

The main course arrived. Peter cut a few bites and then paused. "I guess I wonder if we should think about adoption. I mean, I can't imagine what our friends would think if we had another baby with Down syndrome. Actually, I can imagine. They'd think we're idiots."

I wanted to protest. *You just said that Penny's birth was purposeful. How could you even think of adoption?* And yet, if I was honest, he was speaking aloud my own concerns. I went around and around inside my head. On the one hand, any suggestion that I wouldn't try to get pregnant again because I didn't want another child with Down syndrome felt like a rejection of Penny. On the other, I didn't want another child with Down syndrome. I was scared enough of what people thought about us now, much less what they would think if it happened again. I shook my head, as if I had been speaking out loud. "It's still highly unlikely that we'd have another child with Down syndrome."

Peter raised his eyebrows. "Highly unlikely doesn't mean anything to me anymore."

I looked away again, my thoughts flashing back to the phone call three years earlier and Peter's mom saying, "I have a tumor in my liver." Grand Penny's cancer had been highly unlikely. She had no history of liver disease or cirrhosis. No hepatitis or intravenous drug use. It just happened. Just like our Penny, with her extra chromosome. It just happened. With no explanation. And it could happen again.

I knew Peter was thinking the same thing, so I said, "There are some things in our lives that are highly unlikely and good."

"Such as?"

"Well, such as meeting in high school and staying together. No one would have predicted that. Or you getting the job at

Lawrenceville with no teaching experience. Or the time we were upgraded to business class when we were flying back from Paris. They were all highly unlikely, too." I was hoping we'd someday think of Penny's extra chromosome in that category, the highly-unlikely-but-nevertheless-good category. Instead of the I'm-so-sad-this-happened-and-why-me category.

Peter sighed. "Well, you aren't getting pregnant anytime soon, right? Let's just see what happens."

I nodded my agreement, but I didn't feel settled after our conversation. The following week, the three of us would head to Philadelphia for our appointment with a genetic counselor, and I knew the topic of other children would come up. I tried to prepare myself. On the phone with Virginia, I rambled about our chances of having another child with an extra chromosome. And I said, "I wouldn't rule out getting pregnant again just because we might have another child with Down syndrome. Having Penny has been good. She's healthy and happy and we love her so much."

And Virginia responded, "Yes, the tragedy for you has been emotional, not physical . . ."

I didn't hear the rest. All I could think was, *You just called my daughter a tragedy.*

Later that same day in a similar conversation, I told another friend that I knew the chance of recurrence. "But," I said, "perhaps the geneticist will be able to tell us something more specific."

My friend responded, "And if you do have a high risk, then you have good options. You can always adopt."

And I immediately thought—*Right. We wouldn't want to risk having another child like Penny.*

I also attended my first of the Friday morning coffees for mothers of young children with Down syndrome. There were four other moms present that day. Penny, the youngest of the children, had fallen asleep on the drive over, and she napped in her car seat carrier for most of the morning. I put together a plate of fruit and a bagel and sat down next to Catherine, whom I remembered from our first meeting at the Arc a few months earlier.

"How's Penny doing?" she asked.

"Pretty well, I think," I said. "She's a really easy baby. I don't have any other kids to compare her to, but still." I shrugged.

"It's a well-kept secret," said Lydia, turning to face us. "Jayden's been much easier than either of his older siblings."

"We are going to CHOP next week to meet with a genetic counselor. Did you all do that?"

Catherine pursed her lips. "Don't expect it be uplifting," she said. "Margaret was diagnosed prenatally, so we saw a genetic counselor then. It was terrible. She told us Margaret had something worse than Down syndrome." Catherine was sitting cross-legged on the floor, and Margaret, now two, played with a set of blocks nearby. "I had an amnio—actually, two amnios—and both showed an absence of her first chromosome. They told me she would die in utero or a few days after birth." She glanced over to Margaret and smiled, but there was anger in her eyes. "We don't believe in abortion, but I also didn't want to traumatize Christopher with a dead little sister. In the end, I couldn't bring myself to do it, and so she was born. The amnio was wrong." She skimmed her hand along the top of the carpet. "The genetic counselors don't know as much as they might think."

The stories flowed from there—Lydia had a good experience with a prenatal diagnosis and was supported by her doctor when she chose to continue the pregnancy. Tears streamed down Alicia's cheeks when she described the day, at seven months' gestation, when the doctors told her Ella had fluid around her lungs, a heart defect, kidney trouble, and signs of Down syndrome. The extra chromosome remained, but none of the health complications were present at birth. "I see it as an answer to prayer," she said, wiping her cheeks.

Samantha let out a loud sigh before she began. "Tim was away on business in Europe. I was eleven weeks pregnant and I got a call from a nurse." She was sitting across from me, but her eyes were focused above my head. "The nurse said I had a one in twelve chance of having a baby with Down syndrome. And then she said I could schedule a procedure for the next morning."

I looked around the room at our children—Penny asleep; Jayden, six months old, happily lying on his back; Elizabeth, Ella, and Margaret smiling and babbling and reaching for toys.

And for a moment I wished we could have known ahead of time, just to say that we had chosen her, like these women—against the advice of the doctors, against the assumptions of the culture. I glanced at Penny again. *I choose to receive you, my child.*

We drove to the appointment a few days later. It was a lovely afternoon—springy and sunny. Penny slept the whole way. It soothed me to look at her peaceful face, to think of her earlier that morning, cooing and smiling and resisting tummy time.

My smile waned as we began to navigate the hospital. Through the parking garage to the elevator to the information desk. Down a hallway and over a bridge. Up the elevator to a receptionist to another receptionist to the waiting area. We were surrounded by children and their families. I tried to keep myself from staring. Still, I catalogued—a child in a wheelchair making grunting noises, a child with a backpack holding tubes that reached under her shirt, a young boy with leg braces, a young girl with facial deformities.

We waited ninety minutes for the doctor. Her appearance surprised me—gray hair, a hint of a mustache, a short, plump body. A gentle demeanor, but she spoke quickly and directly. She lay Penny on the crisp white paper of her examination table and started to manipulate her arms and legs. Then she flipped through Penny's chart, scanning my handwritten answers to the form she had provided.

She handed Penny back to Peter, almost as an afterthought, her eyes directed toward the form.

"Okay. First things first. See her eyes? She has an extra fold of skin. It's called an epicanthal fold. And you may have noticed the line across her palm? And the fact that she does some tongue-thrusting? Those are all consistent with a diagnosis of Down syndrome. I know you already have her karyotype, but part of this visit is to offer official confirmation. Your daughter has trisomy 21. So there it is. Good news is that her muscle tone is good. Her home environment is good. And her karyotype indicates that this isn't a case of translocation, so your risk of recurrence is 1 percent and increases with age."

I sat up straighter in my chair. Had I noticed the line across Penny's palm? I wanted to tell her that I had memorized that palm, the creases in her elbows, the dimples in her pudgy cheeks . . .

"Now," she said. "The bad news. Down syndrome means mental retardation."

I interrupted, "Does her physical development tell us anything about her mental ability?"

"No. Typically individuals with Down syndrome have an IQ that falls between 50 and 75, but you won't know where she is until she's older, between the ages of two and three. It is rare for them to have an IQ below 50, which would mean she wouldn't be able to dress herself or toilet. It is also rare to have an IQ above 75. Somewhere around 70 brings with it semi-independence. Even then, she'll have trouble with problem solving and with numbers. As a teenager she might be able to walk herself to school, for instance, but if there was ever a detour, she wouldn't know how to get home. Or, for example, one girl I see with Down syndrome can do addition, but only by counting it out on her fingers."

She said, "You should also know that your risk of having another child with Down syndrome is 1 in 100, and that it increases as you age."

I held back from saying she was repeating herself and instead asked, "If I did have another child with Down syndrome, do we know whether that child would be as healthy as Penny?"

She shook her head, holding her clipboard tight to her chest. "No. There is no guarantee whatsoever. And I will say that having two children with special needs can put a great strain on a family. If you get pregnant again, I recommend an amniocentesis."

I couldn't bring myself to ask her why. *Because we would certainly terminate a pregnancy if we discovered we were having another child with Down syndrome? Because we were irresponsible to bring this child into the world?* I didn't want to explain that for us the choice came before conception. That had we known about Penny's trisomy 21 even on the first day of her life as an embryo, we would have kept her. That we would do the same again. Because we believed there was purpose in her life, as she was.

On the car ride home I curled up in a ball in the passenger seat, hugging my knees toward my chest. "I just want good stories," I said to Peter. "I want to hear that this kid with Down syndrome loves the tuba and this other one loves playing golf with his dad and this one had a hard time with spelling but loves to dance. Or whatever it is. I don't want statistics and predictions of who she will never be. I just want stories."

That night, we put Penny in her swing while we ate dinner. She giggled and her eyes got wide as the lights over her head flashed—red, yellow, blue. I thought about all the ways she was already telling us about herself. The frowns when a dog barked nearby, the cries when she needed attention or rest or food, the inquisitive look when she sucked her fingers, the smiles when Peter or I came near.

After dinner, as we were clearing the dishes, Louis Armstrong came on the radio. Peter pulled my arm and said, "Shall we dance?" He twirled me around the kitchen, dips and spins and our bodies pressed against one another with my cheek resting against his chest, the warmth of his hand upon the small of my back.

And then he whispered, “I need to let Penny cut in for a minute.” He lifted her out of the swing, all nine pounds of her, and held her against his body. Her eyes sparkled as he twirled her around.

It was still hard for me to believe that she wouldn’t solve math problems or read literature. And yet it was easy to believe that she would rush to a friend, or even a stranger, in need. Easy to believe that she would continue to bring light and life. And it was getting easier to believe that, as time went on, she would tell me the stories I needed to hear.

I cringe when people say God chose us to be her parents or that He picked the perfect family for her to be a part of. I resist these statements because they only have to do with us being wonderful, with pressure to stay that way. She, I hope and pray, will be blessed by us, but I also know she will be a blessing to us, an answer to prayers that we be broken of our pride, that we become more real . . .

January 2006

10

For all my years of Christian piety, a few months after Penny was born, I still had trouble talking to God. It had always been easier for me to think about things than actually pray about them. And for a time, I hadn't felt a need to pray. Other people could, and did, pray for me since I couldn't seem to muster the energy, or the faith, to approach God on my own. Even though I hadn't set foot inside our church, I passively and gratefully accepted intercession, in the same way I received casseroles and baked chicken and meatloaf. But as the hours of daylight increased, and spring began to woo me with breezes that smelled earthy and warm, I realized that when it came to God, I was trapped in a barren winter. I wanted things to change.

I called Virginia for advice. "I'm stuck," I said, and described my situation.

"I'm not sure I would call it stuck," she replied. "I think this is just fallow ground."

I wrote her comment in my journal in hopes that she was right. *Maybe God will do something with this emptiness. Maybe someday I'll care about work or intellectual discussions or politics. Maybe I won't always think about Down syndrome all the time. Maybe someday I'll feel like myself again.*

But I also needed to stop imagining that one day I would wake up and return to life-as-usual. It still surprised me really, that Penny had Down syndrome and that Down syndrome was permanent. It wasn't as if a doctor would ever say about her extra chromosome, "It was touch-and-go for a while there, but now we're out of the woods." No, the woods—as vast and beautiful and menacing and fascinating as they might be—were home now. We were there to stay.

Before Penny's birth, I usually joined Peter for the early part of his evenings on duty. Every Tuesday night, he would eat dinner with the boys and then sit downstairs or roam the halls during check-in and study hours and lights-out. He would be gone from 5:30 until midnight. In the fall we had often strolled across campus together, fielding comments from friends about my rapidly expanding midsection, waving hello to kids who had lived in our house the year before, catching up with each other about the details of the past day. But once Penny was born, I stayed in. I told myself it was for her—it was too cold to walk outside at night, and her immune system was more fragile than those of other newborns, and I didn't want to disrupt the nighttime routine we were establishing. But these were convenient excuses. In truth, the walls of our apartment became a refuge for me, a sanctuary.

Inside, I knew what to do. Outside, even for something as simple as a walk to the dining hall, I was afraid. I worried about bumping into one of Peter's colleagues at the salad bar. I imagined their questions: *Why is she so small? Why does her tongue stick out of her mouth? Is it a mild case?* And I wasn't sure I could handle seeing all the other young families with kids bounding from table to table, talking and walking and growing up, doing all the things I was afraid Penny might not ever be able to do.

It was easier to stay home. It was safe. But it had begun to suffocate me.

So one Tuesday night that spring, I brought Penny downstairs to the common room. It was almost time for her to go to sleep. She wore lavender pajamas with white flowers, and her hair, wet from the bath, stuck out over her ears. Peter's laptop sat on the worn green sofa, though he was nowhere to be seen. Two boys lounged in poses of procrastination—a leg slung over the arm of a chair, feet extended upon a coffee table. There was Matt—blond hair and a serious face, with the gait of an athlete. And Joseph, from Brooklyn, still outgrowing his freckles and round cheeks. They each played a varsity sport and took rigorous courses that would put them on the road toward an Ivy League university. I took a seat in an upholstered wing chair and perched Penny on my lap, facing out.

"Hi, Penny," Matt said, with a wave.

"Hi, Matt," I answered, moving her hand up and down.

He smiled. "How is she?"

"She's great," I said, resting my palms on her warm little legs. "We've started physical therapy, and the therapist says she's doing great, too."

"Why does she need therapy?"

I nodded, relieved that he had asked a question I could answer. "She has low muscle tone. It makes her kind of floppy, and it makes it harder for her to sit up and to walk."

Joseph was listening now, along with two others who had wandered into the room as we talked. He asked, "Once you get through all the physical stuff, she'll be normal?"

His tone was so sweet, and his expression so earnest, I hesitated just a minute before responding. My eyes wandered. Decades ago, this room had been the spot where the boys gathered with their housemaster every evening for tea and cookies to discuss the events of the day. It had since lost its formality, but reminders of the past hung on the walls in the forms of placards and black-and-white photos, and the room held the contemporary marks of the highly educated—the backpacks filled with massive textbooks, copies of the *New York Times* and *Wall Street Journal* spread out upon the coffee table.

I faced Joseph and said, "We know two things for sure. Penny's physical development will be delayed, and she'll have mental retardation."

He looked down and said, "That's really hard." When he raised his head again, his eyes were wet.

I tried to keep my voice steady as I said, "You know, it is hard, but I think it's good, too. I've always valued intelligence too much, I think. And even that—intelligence . . . There are so many forms of intelligence. Penny might not be book smart when she grows up, but I'm sure she'll teach us a lot."

A crease appeared between Joseph's eyebrows. "But what will she be like when she's older?"

I tried to see Penny from the eyes of these students. They had watched Peter take her in the crook of his arm and carry her around the house like a football. They had seen him dance with his daughter and sing to her and call her beautiful. Peter rarely talked about muscle tone or IQs, so I realized what I was saying came as a surprise. "Let's just say she won't be going to Lawrenceville," I replied gently, voicing out loud this thought that knocked on the door of my mind every day as I looked out our window at the students walking across the grass.

"I bet she will," Matt said, leaning forward. "I know a girl from home with Down syndrome, and she takes AP classes."

Joseph, more relaxed now, said, "I know a kid whose IQ is only 96, but he's really smart."

I didn't tell Matt he had to be wrong about the girl from home. I didn't tell Joseph that mental retardation is considered an IQ of 70 or below. I just held Penny, with her back pressing against my stomach and her hands clutching my index fingers, and her hair that smelled like honey underneath my chin. And I saw these boys—who had begun to love her—I saw them start to want the world for her. To insist that with the advantages of America and financial security and boarding school and all the rest, she would not be different. She would be just like them. Right?

But she wouldn't be just like them.

I said, "You know, for all of my life, I have relied upon being smart. I've always been the kid who could read and write faster than anyone else and get good grades and all that. And it's not a bad thing that I like being smart. But it is a bad thing if all I value is intelligence, and if I can't care about or relate to people who aren't the same as me. I don't think Penny will be intelligent in the same way that I am, but I think she'll have other abilities—emotional, or artistic, or just an ability to love people."

They nodded as I talked, but the sadness returned to their eyes.

Peter had walked back into the room while I was speaking, and I stood to greet him.

"Hello, beautiful," he said, with a kiss for me and then another for our daughter.

I smiled and said, "It's time for bed."

Once upstairs, with Penny asleep in her crib, I lay down, hands behind my head. The conversation had pushed me into memories of my own days away at school. I had rarely sat around and talked with faculty members or gotten to know their families. I had been too busy. All those papers, all those good grades. I remembered when I received my early acceptance letter to Princeton. It was over Christmas vacation, so I was home alone when the mail came and could only celebrate by myself. I didn't cry out or jump up and down. I just let a grin spread across my face, delighted, but also self-satisfied, as if I had known what the letter would say. As if I deserved it.

That was the thing. I thought I deserved it. I thought that all the hours of studying and forgoing social events in favor of homework and doing independent projects with teachers—I thought my achievements were due only to hard work. But I had no doubt Penny would work just as hard as I had, maybe harder. And she would never go to Princeton. It wasn't just about hard work. It was about background and genetics and opportunity. My life wasn't something I deserved. It was a gift.

A few days later, Penny was lying on her back with toys hanging overhead. She screwed up her face, eyeing the red and purple rings. Then she moved her left hand, first in an arc from her ear to the dangling circles above, and then again with a swipe from the side. She grasped the rings and held on. I swelled with pride.

But as soon as she let go of the ring, with hardly a pause to clap for her accomplishments, I let my thoughts go. *Maybe she will be the exception. Maybe she'll be the child with Down syndrome who beats the odds. Maybe she won't be delayed. Maybe we don't need to think about legal guardianship when she turns eighteen or integrated versus self-contained classrooms or social services or occupational therapy.*

My thoughts moved so quickly away from Penny, from that moment of triumph to fear. Just like that first day in the hospital when Penny was in the nursery. Out of my sight she had become a concept, an abstraction, rather than a living gift, a child, our little girl.

All through my pregnancy, I had compared my experience to "what the books said," and it always relieved me when the two lined up. And as soon as Penny grabbed that ring, I wanted to reach over to the bookshelf and pull out a chart that told me when a typical child would start to grab with accuracy. Or to open a recent acquisition, *Gross Motor Skills for Children with Down Syndrome*, and see whether she was ahead of the curve. But before I opened either book, I stopped to study Penny's face, the cheeks that looked like two mounds of dough, the long eyelashes that had started to curl, the eyebrows that had changed from blond to brown.

I reached out my hand. She grabbed hold with her fingers, and I tried to believe that I didn't need books to tell me what I was seeing when I looked at our daughter. All I needed was to know that she was developing—that last week she swatted and today she grabbed. That she could lift her head a few seconds longer. That she had begun to enjoy sitting on my lap and looking around the room. That her eyes followed toys. That she could hold on to her rattle.

It seemed as though every day another event occurred—she smiled, I propped her upright on the couch and she didn't fall over, she turned her head at the sound of my voice. And every day I puzzled through pride and love that was somehow coupled with fear and sadness. We strolled around campus, and I noted out loud the life emerging all around us. After the crocuses came the daffodils, their cheery heads waving in the dappled sunlight. In May, with Penny four months old, the dogwoods and cherry blossoms bloomed and their petals rained down. I started to pray. Just a very simple prayer. *Lord Jesus, I want to know you again. I want to believe.*

It took me a while to think my prayer would ever be answered. But then one day, four senior girls came to visit.

Two years earlier, as sophomores, they had asked me to lead them in a Bible study. Once a week, early in the morning, they had shown up at our door. They knew to let themselves into the kitchen and start making breakfast, and then they piled into our living room and peppered me with questions about God and Jesus and the church, sex and drinking and boyfriends and marriage, other religions, politics. We had talked about alcoholism and the death of a friend and eating disorders, and they had watched my body change throughout my pregnancy. They had shed their own tears when Penny was born. This was the first time in months that all four of them had been in our apartment together.

Eliza picked up Penny's birth announcement as soon as she walked through the door. She flopped onto the sofa to take a look. I had just sent the announcements out, even though I had selected them months earlier—lime green with bright blue letters. We included a photo of Penny at three weeks old. In the photo her eyes were closed and her hands had snuck up to just underneath her chin, as though she were praying.

Audrey peered over Eliza's shoulder to see the card and photo. With a sigh of contentment she said, "It's perfect."

Eliza nodded. "Perfect." And then she looked around the room—the mantel filled with family photos, the wall-to-wall bookcases, the painting of Venetian gondolas over the fireplace. "It's all perfect," she said, with a vague sweep of her hand. "The pictures, the furniture, the paintings, your family, everything."

"It is," Catherine said, insistent. "You have the perfect life."

Of all the things for these girls to say—these kind, athletic, sweet, smart girls—a perfect family? A perfect life? My life was as imperfect as it had ever been. There were days I couldn't find the time to take a shower, much less return phone calls or put the dishes in the dishwasher. There was the disorder of my thoughts, the questions for God, the tears. And then there was Penny. The language surrounding Down syndrome suggested a special state of imperfection—abnormal, birth defect, cell division gone wrong.

I wanted to ask what it was that made them say we were perfect. Was it just the surface? The lovely things and the college degrees and the smiling people in photographs? Or was there something more, something of substance? I took a deep breath, as if I was about to respond at length, but "Thank you" was all I said.

After the girls headed out, I sat with Penny on the floor of the playroom. She raised her hands in the air and studied them, flexing her wrists and wiggling her fingers. I couldn't stop thinking about Catherine's words. It wasn't the first time my life had been called perfect. When I was a child on vacation, sometimes strangers would notice the four blond girls who were well-behaved and seemed to enjoy one another, and make the comment, "What a perfect family." And it had continued when I got into college, and then when I married my high school sweetheart and we went on to work together for a nonprofit organization and then he got exactly the job he wanted and I got into exactly the Master's program I wanted. Perfect family. Perfect marriage. Perfect life.

I took Penny's hands and started to go through the steps of infant massage. My thumb in the arch of her foot, fingers on top, rotating her ankle left, then right. My thumb pushing against the sole of her foot, heel to toes. My hands on her legs, twisting gently, as if I were wringing out a towel. All the time, thinking, the muscles of my own body tight with concentration, as if I needed to wade through the weeds of memories to get to the clear water of thoughts. As if there was something worth seeing up ahead, if only I could make a way.

I interrupted the massage to pull a Bible from the shelf. Penny gazed up at me as I flipped through its pages to find the verse that had come to mind from Matthew's gospel. Jesus said, "Be perfect, therefore, as your heavenly father is perfect." It seemed such a strange command. Jesus must have known that we would never be perfect, if by "perfect" He meant without flaw, without needs, without hurts or wants. It was counterintuitive, even, to try to be just like God. Wasn't that the first sin, the very thing that caused Adam and Eve's banishment from the garden?

"Hold on, sweet girl," I said to Penny with a kiss on her forehead as I retrieved my Greek dictionary. The root of the word, I discovered, was *telos*. It could be translated as "perfect," but it could also be translated, "wholeness, completion, the end for which you were created."

And there was Penny—floppy limbs and ears filled with fluid and eyes that reminded me of deep pools of still water—there was Penny. Catherine had called us a perfect family, although of course we weren't that. We would never be that. Still, I wondered whether Penny had brought us closer to becoming the family we were created to be.

I put aside the Bible and the dictionary, laughing at myself a little bit. A seed had been planted in that fallow ground, through a comment from a high school student. Through a dictionary. Through my daughter. I lay down on the floor next to Penny. A shaft of sunshine warmed my shoulder and bathed her face in light. She grabbed hold of my index finger and I whispered, "Hello, beautiful girl. And thank you."

Penny smiles all the time. She giggled yesterday when I bounced her up and down. She rolls and sucks her fingers and coos and looks us in the eye. She pulls her legs into the air and grabs at rings and clothing and toys. She is beautiful and sweet and we love love love her.

Can she live a full life without ever solving a quadratic equation? Without reading Dostoyevsky? I'm pretty sure she can. Can I live a full life without learning to cherish and welcome those in this world who are different from me? I'm pretty sure I can't.

April 2006

11

Peter found me in the living room, curled up in one of the armchairs we had inherited from his mother. He flopped on the couch across from me and put his hands behind his neck. "You are never going to believe this."

I put my book down. "What is it?"

He shook his head, a bemused expression on his face. "I feel like we've just become members of an exclusive club, and I didn't even know we'd applied."

I waited for more. He had just come home from an all-school meeting. Penny had been asleep for over an hour. I was drowsy myself, reclined with a glass of wine and a book.

Peter sat forward, elbows on knees. "So I knew the speaker tonight was the grandfather of one of my squash players. But it was weird, because a couple different people told me that he really wanted to meet me and talk to me after his speech. I was thinking about how I didn't know I'd made such a difference in this girl's life and how I must be such an amazing coach, and then he gets to the part in his speech where he talks about being a senator who helped write the Americans with Disabilities Act because he has a son with Down syndrome!"

Peter's energy was contagious. I straightened up and sat cross-legged, like a kid at story time, waiting for the tale's climax. He said, "First I had to laugh at myself, since the fact that he wanted to talk to me had nothing to do with my abilities as a squash coach or a teacher or anything. I got singled out because of Penny. All of a sudden, it was a privilege to be the one with the daughter with Down syndrome."

"So what did he say to you?"

"Well, he shook my hand and slapped me on the back. He's a big man—taller than me. And he said, 'Congratulations!'" Peter shook his head. "I don't think anyone else has been able to say that so definitively. And he talked about his son. I don't even know what he said. It was just clear that he was proud of him. I mean, really, I felt like I walked into the most exclusive country club in the country, but it wasn't because I had all sorts of money or the right résumé. It was because of Penny."

He stood up. "I've got to go give her a kiss."

"Don't wake her up!" I called, as he bounded down the hallway. But I wouldn't have minded if he had. I thought back to that first day in the hospital, when Peter had been encompassed by the darkness of Penny's diagnosis, when he thought he would never be proud of her, never be able to love her, never think she was beautiful. I thought about how we had been afraid other people would pity us. And I remembered, as he was coming out of the pain of it all, he had said, "The highs will be higher and the lows will be lower." I had known it was true at the time, even though I couldn't anticipate the ways his words would play themselves out.

I heard Peter's footsteps again and looked up. "One more thing," he said.

I nodded.

"So the boys in the house?" He waved his arms to indicate the dorm of thirty boys outside our apartment door. "You know how they raised money for a well in a village in India last year? They just told me that this year they want to raise money for Down syndrome, wherever we want it to go."

I thought about Matt and Joseph and all the other boys we saw every day. With a catch in my throat, I said, "That's wonderful."

Peter kissed me before he headed back out into the dorm for a house meeting. I picked up a book on the coffee table, a gift that had arrived earlier that day. It was filled with photographs and stories of real people with Down syndrome—people playing on sports teams and a young man who became a deacon in his church, stories about boy scouts, volunteers, writers, artists, musicians. As I flipped through the pages, the images startled me. I thought—these kids are adorable, beautiful, just right. And I couldn't believe my own response. I had a picture in my brain of what a person with Down syndrome looked like, but it didn't match these faces. Where did my picture come from? Certainly not from personal interaction. From a composite of the handful of ads for the Special Olympics I had seen over the course of my life? Or perhaps I was starting to see beyond the common characteristics to the individuals. Perhaps it was as if I had moved to Korea and finally was learning to see distinctions among faces and body types instead of a mass of people who all looked the same to me. I closed the book with a small sigh and a smile. Peter was right. The highs were higher.

But with beauty came pain. In mid-May we drove to the Children's Hospital of Philadelphia again, this time so that tubes could be inserted in Penny's ears. The procedure itself was easy. I had been warned by my friends that the hardest part of the day would be watching Penny, all ten pounds of her, wheeled away on a stretcher. In our case, the doctor cradled our daughter in her arms and carried her away. An hour later, she was done. I cringed to see the bruises on Penny's hands, purple reminders of what had happened behind the scenes. But her recovery went well. She slept for seventeen of the next twenty hours and woke up her usual happy self.

There wasn't much to worry about when it came to Penny. I had learned the statistics—the higher rate of celiac disease and leukemia, the impoverished immune system, the chance of early onset Alzheimer's. But right now I had a daughter who was flourishing, a little girl who mimicked my facial expressions and threw her head back in laughter at her dad and found herself utterly fascinated by her own right hand. What troubled me was the suffering that countless other children, other families, endured—the miscarriages, the deformities, the kids who never talked or walked or bathed or dressed themselves, the kids born into pain, the babies who died in the womb, the three-year-old with a brain tumor. And then I heard about a little boy with Down syndrome who had been born prematurely. He had died when he was five months old. He had never come home from the hospital. Theirs was the suffering I could not explain. Theirs was the pain I could not imagine having to bear.

Now that I had seen those families—in the elevator, in the waiting room, in the books and online sites for parents of children with disabilities—now I had to wrestle with their pain. Either there was no God and natural selection worked her purposeless work and some of us passed along our genes and others failed and died trying, or God did exist and God's creation was broken, but still glorious—every piece and person in it. I saw the brokenness more clearly in those with an extra chromosome, but I was starting to understand that their brokenness was no different from my own.

One night at dinner, I asked Peter again, "If you could take away Penny's extra chromosome, would you?"

He wiped his mouth with his napkin and tapped his fingers together. "I don't know."

I nodded. My answer was changing, too. "When it comes to Penny, I think I'm starting to understand why she has Down syndrome. Or at least to understand that she is who she should be, and that who she should be includes Down syndrome. I wouldn't take away her extra chromosome because it might change her—her eye color or her smile or her personality. Saying I wanted to take away the extra chromosome would be like saying I wanted to take her away. But I can't come to terms with some of the other disabilities and illnesses I see. Driving back and forth to the hospital—I just can't stand how many kids are suffering and dying every day. I can't understand how there is any purpose or goodness to it."

Peter chewed slowly. "Well, there have always been thousands of kids in cancer wards."

"But until your child has cancer and lives, and your new friend's child dies, you can ignore those questions or keep them theoretical. Before, I didn't have to think about those kids. Now I do."

Penny's birth had caused me to rethink everything, start to finish. I remembered the feeling just after she was born, of waiting for the tsunami, waiting for the wave to crash. It was as if I had been swept out to sea in the hospital, but I hadn't drowned. Now I found myself on the beach again, but the shore was different. I didn't have my landmarks anymore.

Peter had called it an exclusive club. I wanted to agree with him, but some days I thought we had become part of a group that was cut off from the rest of the world. There were moments like the one we had in a friend's living room. A kid from their neighborhood had come to visit. Penny sat on my lap. He looked at me and said, "Why does she look Chinese?"

I felt as though my heart had stopped and reset. I said, heat rising to my cheeks, "Because she has an extra fold of skin around her eyes."

"Oh."

People noticed Penny. They noticed the epicanthal fold. They noticed her tongue. They noticed her floppy limbs. But they also noticed her attentiveness, the blue eyes speckled with light, her eagerness to smile. And again and again I heard the astonishment in their voices when they said, "She's adorable!" "She's so beautiful!" "She's so alert!" I tried to remember that I had been surprised by it, too.

In June, on the afternoon of our seventh wedding anniversary, Peter and I took Penny into New York City. Months earlier, my aunt, who had trained as a physical therapist in college, had given me a book called *Yoga for the Special Child*. I coaxed Penny's body into the poses nearly every day, and I had discovered that the book's author would be in the city for a training session. The three of us entered a studio with about twenty women sitting cross-legged. Sonia Sumar, the instructor, took Penny from Peter and invited us to sit back and watch.

I could feel the anticipation in my chest, the excuses rising in case Penny didn't respond the way she was supposed to—*It's nap time . . . She's never been in the city before . . . She's only five months old . . .* But then Sonia began to chant and breathe rapidly through her nose. Penny giggled. She giggled again, entranced. And soon enough, there was my daughter, happily complying as a stranger manipulated her limbs, turned her torso for a twist, and then laid her on her tummy with arms extended. Then onto her back, and before long Penny's hips were in the air in a perfect impression of bridge pose. Out of the corner of my eye, I saw Peter wipe away a tear.

Twenty minutes later, it was over. The three of us crowded the stairwell outside the studio so Penny could nurse.

"I was prepared to be cynical," Peter said.

I couldn't contain my smile. "I know."

He exhaled loudly. "But, man. Just seeing her with Sonia. It was so beautiful." He kissed Penny on the crown of her head.

I finished nursing and put Penny over my shoulder to rub her back. Just then a woman rounded the corner. Her black curly hair fell past her elbows. She paused to look at Penny. She made faces for a moment and then declared, as if it were a pronouncement, "This child is surrounded by the most glorious light." And then she walked up the stairs.

A moment later, another woman arrived. She nodded to Peter and me, but then sat down next to Penny and began speaking to her in Italian. After we listened to her lilting phrases for a few minutes, she looked up at us. "You have a beautiful daughter."

"Thank you," we murmured.

"But may I ask why you're here?"

I gestured toward the classroom. "We brought Penny because they're teaching yoga instructors how to assist kids with disabilities."

"Does she have disabilities?"

I stroked Penny's hair. "She has Down syndrome."

"Ah." A smile spread across the woman's face slowly, as imperceptibly as early morning sunlight reaches over the horizon. "I used to teach children with Down syndrome how to swim. What a gift."

"That's what everyone says," Peter replied.

"I will tell you one story. It was a day for Special Olympics competitions. And this wasn't in the pool. It was outside on the track. The kids were, oh, I don't know, eight years old. They started running. And one of them fell down. And the rest of the kids stopped running. Every one of them stopped running and went over to help the one who had fallen. They finished the race as a group, helping the one who had been hurt." She pushed herself up from the step. "Well, *mia cara*," she said to Penny, "it was a pleasure to meet you." She extended her hand to each of us and went on her way.

As we drove home, all I could think about was her story. Even as an eight-year-old, it wouldn't have crossed my mind to abandon the goal of winning the race in order to help another participant. I said to Peter, "You know, there are all these people who try to console me about Penny by telling me the 'normal' things she'll be able to do. They tell me about a young man with Down syndrome they know who takes a bus to work every day. And I think, *That's supposed to be good news, that my daughter won't be able to drive a car but might have a job?*" I shook my head, gazing out the window at the cars passing by. "I know that there are plenty of reasons to be encouraged. But for me, the thought that Penny might one day walk herself to work is not one of them.

It's the stories like the one we just heard. It's the thought that she might teach me to slow down, to love deeply, to compete less, to live more fully—those are the stories that bring hope."

Peter said, "It's not just that she'll teach us, but I think she'll be the one to do those things. She will be the one who stops for the injured kid. She'll be the one we admire."

He reached out and took my hand in his. And we drove home, this family of three.

Penny's eyes are still very blue. Her iris has two distinct rings. The inner ring that surrounds her pupil is gray-blue and it bleeds into the outer ring, the blue of deep, still water. They look like pieces of blown glass. It's ironic that those eyes—those slanted, epicanthal-fold eyes—are so distinctly beautiful. I am always surprised because she isn't beautiful-even-though-she-has-Down-syndrome. She simply is beautiful.

At the same time, I find myself angry that Penny has this extra chromosome. Some of that anger has to do with the problems it may cause her, that life might be harder for her than it would otherwise be. But much of my anger comes because life with a child with Down syndrome is probably going to be harder for me. . . .

June 2006

12

Halfway through Penny's first year, as she began to try solid foods and learned how to form spit bubbles, as she mimicked our facial expressions and started to babble, as she laughed with her head thrown back and her mouth wide open, we moved to Connecticut for the summer. My parents had a beach house on the shore, and we were invited to live there for the two months of Peter's summer vacation. Our days were filled with people—Penny's aunts, her grandparents, great-aunts and uncles, even three great-grandparents. She loved the attention. If she cried, all she needed was for one of us to take her outside so she could feel the wind on her face. If the air was still, we soon discovered that music soothed her within minutes. As her Aunt Elly said, " 'Let's Go Fly a Kite' is as good as Valium." Penny heard us sing it dozens of times.

It was a summer of laughter. One day we sat outside on the cement porch eating sandwiches, with Penny nestled into her Nana's lap, and I commented that Penny's face was a perfect circle. "She could be a pumpkin," Brooks said, and Penny giggled as much as the rest of us. Almost every time someone leaned in to kiss her, she grabbed their hair or chin or nose and they found themselves smiling at the greeting. As she learned to eat—peaches, mushy cereal, peas—she also learned to communicate when she was all done by spitting out the final mouthful and splattering anyone in her way. She sat on a rocking chair and bounced herself back and forth, alternately opening her mouth wide, sticking out her tongue, and experimenting with sounds—*babadadada-ahh*—to the claps and exclamations of anyone nearby.

We settled into a routine. I spent the mornings writing while Peter put Penny down for a nap. He dropped her off with me when it was time to nurse, and then most days he dressed her in a bright pink bathing suit and hat and took her to the water's edge. The little waves hugged her legs and she fingered sand and rocks and shells. I joined them for lunch and played with Penny until it was time for her afternoon nap. We ate summer tomatoes and peaches and squash and picked zinnias from my grandmother's garden.

Up to this point, the most constant emotion I felt about Penny's diagnosis was sadness. I had thought that the salt air, the presence of family, the laughter and wind and music, would turn my sadness to delight. The sorrow did begin to dissipate, but only to make room for anger. I had started praying again, and my prayer took the form of words I had been taught not to say when I was a little girl. In no uncertain terms, I expressed my anger to God. Anger that Penny had Down syndrome. Anger that other children suffered and died. Anger that there was a cloud of uncertainty over the health of any of our future babies. Anger that I knew the directions to the Children's Hospital by heart. Anger that I had to spend time learning about muscle tone and reading books about therapy. But most of all, I was angry at the thought that Penny had Down syndrome because we needed to be taught a lesson.

I had heard it from friends starting that first weekend in the hospital. That God gave "these" children to people who needed them, who needed to learn patience and compassion and a different set of values. It made me even more angry to realize that they might be right. When I considered why I might "need" a child who took longer to learn how to speak, to walk, to read, to tie her shoes, to add and subtract, I could give a list of very good reasons. It would be good for me to be forced not to compete and compare myself, my child, my parenting, to my friends and their children. As an achievement-oriented, impatient individual, it already felt like a rebuke whenever Penny didn't "hit a milestone on time." Penny's condition highlighted my own condition as a person with many flaws and failings that I would rather not see. Her existence forced me to recognize ugly parts of myself.

But there was another explanation given to us about why Penny had Down syndrome. We were told that "they" were only given to very special people, as if we had passed some cosmic parenting exam and found ourselves at the top of the heap. I always wanted to retort, "If that's the case, then why do so many women with a prenatal diagnosis of Down syndrome abort their babies? Were they singled out as special parents, too?" Or, with a slightly softer tone, I wanted to ask, "You say they are a gift, but do you long for a child with Down syndrome?"

For some, it seemed that Penny was a rebuke to our perfectionist tendencies, our overachieving ways. For others, she was a reward. And yet all this talk seemed to me to come at the expense of our daughter. In either scenario, her existence was all about us.

That summer, we slept with the windows open, hoping to coax a breeze into our room. I would awaken while it was still dark to the cries of the birds outside. Once, I dreamed that Penny climbed out of her crib and began to crawl across the floor. And in the dream, I felt relieved. Not only was she able to crawl, but she surprised me and everyone else by crawling early. Another night, I dreamed that Penny and I were taking a walk. From her stroller, she pointed and said, "Squirrel." Again, relief washed over me. But then I lay in bed chastising my subconscious for wanting her to be different than she was. As the darkness turned to the gray light of early morning, I reminded myself that most kids with Down syndrome didn't crawl until they were nearly two, and many didn't speak until they were three or four.

Some hardly spoke at all, even as adults. And the question remained—did I recognize the value of my daughter independent of her accomplishments, or would she need to prove herself to me?

In the light of morning, the nighttime demons scuttled away. Every day brought with it cause for excitement. She ate a whole jar of peas! She tried to pull herself up on my hands! Her hearing test showed only a mild loss!

My parents' house proved an easy rest stop for anyone traveling the I-95 corridor, and we welcomed visits from friends throughout the summer. In August, Virginia and her two children arrived. I hadn't seen her in person in nearly a year, since she had hosted a baby shower for me and Peter. She looked the same as ever—cropped blond hair, the body of a college-aged girl, a bright smile for me and bright eyes that landed on Penny. She reached out her arms and held Penny on her hip. "Hello, my friend!"

Penny blinked.

Virginia crouched down to introduce Penny to her own children, aged two and four. Penny's head moved from one to the next until her face broke out in a big smile.

"I think she likes you," I said.

Within an hour, we had piled towels, shovels, water bottles, and suntan lotion into the base of Penny's stroller, and we set out for the beach. Penny wore a floppy white hat with stencils of animals around the brim. I lay a towel on the sand and plopped her into its midst. I was ready to ease her onto her back, but she stayed upright.

"Virginia, look!"

Virginia turned her head from helping her kids start a sand castle.

"She's sitting up!" I cried. And she was. Penny was sitting up on her own. I hovered around her until, a few minutes later, she toppled over and landed on the towel I had propped behind her. She grasped both feet with her hands and smiled into the sunlight. And then she did it again. And again.

"She's not supposed to be able to sit up," I said, scanning a chart in my head. "I think it's supposed to be a couple months from now."

Virginia leaned close to Penny and tickled her round belly. "Yes, sweet girl, you are just so strong and amazing, aren't you?"

We sat side by side. I looked out across the water, taking in the rocks I had scraped my knees against as a kid, the seaweed clustered along the high-tide line, the sailboats in the distance. I held the thrill of Penny's accomplishment inside my chest, as if it were a butterfly cupped in my hands. I didn't want to let it go, and yet I was afraid I would damage those fragile wings.

And then Virginia pulled herself away from Penny and laughed. "Six months old is a perfectly normal time to sit up!"

I laughed, too, although something started to knock around in the back of my brain, some discomfort I wanted to shake off.

Virginia went on, her smile wide, her tone light: "So Penny will get Cs and Bs in school instead of making the honor roll. And maybe she'll play JV instead of varsity. And I bet it will still be really hard for you and Peter."

I forced a smile. She was trying to encourage me, but I was already second-guessing my pride in Penny's newest accomplishment. I had been trying to resist the temptation to put everything on a timeline, to measure and quantify my daughter. And I resisted Virginia's words, too. Penny wasn't going to get Bs and Cs or play JV sports. At least, I had to get used to the idea that she wouldn't.

I picked up a handful of sand and let it run through my fingers. It was coarse, with specks of black that stuck to my skin. I was grateful for my sunglasses, for the distractions of kids making sand castles.

Penny toppled over and I summoned a cheery voice. "Do you need a rest, sweet girl? Come sit with Mama." She sat in my lap holding her hands together, raising them every so often, as if to applaud, when she spotted a bird or a little wave crashed on the shore.

Later that night as I lay in bed, I argued with God—*We have plenty of friends who are equally driven and who have equally high expectations for their families. Why are we the only ones with a child with special needs?* I realized then that I was angry not at our solitary status but at the presumption altogether. Virginia's words stood as a summary of a host of comments that had come in the guise of explanation and consolation, and I had repeated those comments to myself. But now I thought, *Am I really so awful—such a controlling perfectionist—that I needed a child with an extra chromosome? Could I not have learned through a typical child?* Nice as it had been to have an answer for Penny's diagnosis, I wasn't satisfied with it any longer.

Around the same time, we were invited to visit two families with adult sons with Down syndrome. First, we spent an afternoon with Buddy. Peter had met his family through Lawrenceville, and they invited us to join them for lunch. Buddy's father opened the door to greet us. He ushered us to the backyard, where the whole family was scattered about. When I first saw Buddy, I felt shy. We were peers of a sort, as I was only two years older. And yet I didn't know what we would find to talk about.

He put me at ease, hand extended. "Nice to meet you!"

We perched Penny upon a glass-topped table, showing off her newfound ability to sit up straight. Buddy tickled her under the chin and sat down nearby. *He looks just like his dad,* I thought. He had a thick neck and big hands. He sat back in his chair for a moment, but soon he sprang to his feet and grabbed a Nerf football.

"Buddy, tell them about your job," his dad said.

His face lit up. "My job? I work in Hartford. At a law firm." He pounded the football against the palm of his hand.

"What do you do there?" Peter asked.

"Oh, you know, errands. I make copies. The people are really nice."

"What do you do when you aren't working?" I asked.

He jumped in place and said, "I'm starting a hip-hop class soon."

"Maybe I'll join you," his dad said.

Buddy spun around. "You aren't energetic enough, Dad."

He wandered away, and his father leaned forward. "He's a great kid. A great kid. The one thing is that he really wants to live on his own. So we're working on that. Right now, he's in an assisted living facility with a few other young men and some aides. We think we're going to be able to arrange for him to have a separate house nearby."

I nodded. It seemed so far away, but even with a six-month-old, social workers and older parents had suggested we start planning for Penny's adult life. They encouraged us to save for the possibility that she would never be self-sufficient. We had recently purchased a run-down summer cottage near my parents' home in Connecticut, and I envisioned it many years into the future, fixed up as a house where we could retire. Maybe Penny would have her own apartment over the garage.

We stayed through lunch, and Buddy and his family all commented on how "well" Penny was doing. I appreciated their encouragement, but what mattered most to me was seeing this family together. Buddy was a brother, a son. He was a young man in his own right, with a big smile and broad shoulders, with slightly garbled speech and a quirky sense of humor.

The following week we met Dave and his parents. He lived alone in a single-story white house near the center of town. I found myself comparing him to Buddy. He was smaller, more subdued. His words were harder to understand. He told us about his love for music, just like Buddy. He talked about his job and his girlfriend. He gave us a tour of his house. At the end of our time together, Penny sat next to him on the couch in his living room. She waved her hands and babbled as if she had a lifetime of stories to tell him. He gazed at her, rapt with attention.

On the drive home I said, "I've never seen Penny respond to anyone like she did to Dave."

Peter shook his head. "I know. It's as if she was able to sense some degree of gentleness or, I don't know, shared chromosomal makeup or something."

"Yeah, but it wasn't the same with Buddy. That's part of what was so good for me in meeting them back to back. I know there were similarities. But they were such individuals. Dave was kind of shy and I could tell that Buddy could be an annoying, loud younger brother sometimes. It's like their families mattered more than anything else in making them who they are."

Peter continued my thought, "And that talking about Down syndrome in general terms isn't all that helpful." He tapped his fingers on the steering wheel. "You know, one of the things I've loved this summer is that the grocery stores around here have baggers with Down syndrome. It's funny. Every time I go to Stop and Shop, I ignore the cashiers because I'm so excited to say hello to the baggers. And before Penny was born, I would never have said, 'I really hope my first child is a grocery bagger when she grows up,' but that's because I just didn't get it. The woman at Stop and Shop and the man at the Big Y—they're both good at their jobs, and they always greet me so nicely. I have to imagine that their lives are just as satisfying as mine is. For Buddy and Dave, same thing. It makes me so happy to be her dad." He glanced in the rearview mirror. "You've shown me a whole new world, my love."

That night, as I continued to work through the thoughts and questions and encounters of the previous week, I remembered another story from John's gospel. In it, Jesus's disciples approached a blind man. But they didn't see him as an individual. They saw him as a theological problem, a rhetorical question. They asked—*Who sinned, this man or his parents, that he was born blind?* I felt as though we had been asked, and that we were asking ourselves, a variation of that question. *Who sinned, Peter or Amy Julia, that this baby was born with Down syndrome? Why did God do this? Is this a punishment, a rebuke?*

Or maybe there was a more contemporary spin to put on it. *Whose genes are screwed up? What environmental factors in Amy Julia's or Peter's life led to this outcome?*

In John's story, Jesus answered His disciples by saying, "Neither this man nor his parents sinned, but this happened that the glory of the Lord might be revealed."

And as much as I wanted order and reasons—as much as I wanted answers, even if those answers included judgment—instead I received this truth: Penny is neither a rebuke nor a reward. She is a child, not a product of sin or of biological happenstance or of any lesson we needed to learn. No. This happened that the glory of God might be revealed.

With that thought, I felt my anger dissolve. I didn't remember my dreams that night. And it wasn't the birds I heard in the morning. It was the babbling sounds of my daughter, awakening me to the day.

On the one hand, Penny has a hole in her heart and she can't roll over and her teeth are crooked and emerging randomly. I get frightened when she gets a cold because her body is more vulnerable to infection. On the other hand, she is sweet and smiley and patient and fun. She gives me kisses and works hard. And somehow it is all intricately bound together—the extra chromosome and the physical difficulties and the sweetness. I used to think it was a trite consolation, along the lines of a date having "a good personality," to say that kids with Down syndrome tend to be mentally and physically delayed and also really loving. But I must have thought that because I didn't value the loving part. Is there something "wrong" with my child? I don't really know. All I can say is that there are many things that are right—exactly right. Crooked teeth and all, exactly right.

October 2006

13

When I was a little girl, my mother often said, "If I could bottle up Elly's laugh and sell it, we'd be millionaires." After that comment I always pictured my baby sister Elly giggling, her curly white-blond hair framing her round cheeks, ready to be released upon a dreary world in need of joy. As summer turned to fall, I started to feel something similar about Penny.

We returned to Lawrenceville for another school year, and I found myself delighted with Penny's every look, every sound, every movement. Now that she could sit up, she did, all day long, like a judge in a courtroom, proper and stern. She was content to observe her surroundings, and she rarely moved around or fell over. If she did find herself on her back, she would pull her feet into her mouth and nibble on her big toes. Most visitors received a big grin and a slobbery kiss, and she usually watched me talk with a friend as if she were taking mental notes on the art of conversation.

She kept learning new things. One day I walked into her room and said, "Good morning, sunshine. Time to get up."

She raised her arms in the air, as if she understood.

She started to turn toward me at the sound of her name. She learned to eat avocado, raspberries, peas. We took our first trip to the grocery store. She began to roll from her tummy to her back. In September, she cut her first tooth.

A few weeks after we returned, I was sitting with Penny in her room, folding clothes. She was nine months old, but the labels on most of her clothing still read "3 to 6 months." I had a prick of nostalgia as I realized she was outgrowing her pink plaid jumper, the pajamas with the frogs on them, the polka-dotted sundress. I tucked them into a bag in the closet as the phone rang.

"Hello?"

"Hi. It's me." It was Virginia.

We exchanged pleasantries for a bit, and then she said, "I just read a novel where one of the characters has Down syndrome."

I stopped folding the laundry and sat down. Penny craned her neck to see me.

Virginia said, "I just wanted to call to say I'm sorry."

"Sorry for what?"

"Well, I just don't think I really got it. How permanent this is. I mean, the character in the book is wonderful, but Down syndrome affects her for her whole life. And I just don't think I understood that very well."

I felt my body relax. "Thanks for calling," I said. I couldn't quite tell her what I was thinking. *Thank you*, and yet at the same time, *Don't be sorry*. "Send me the book if you get a chance. I'd love to read it, too."

It was strange to realize that when I looked to the future, Down syndrome no longer felt ominous. It just felt unknown. Sure, it would impact Penny, and us, for the rest of our lives, but I didn't know exactly *how* it would impact us. It was only the inconsequential things that were different now, like introducing a straw instead of a sippy cup because sippy cups increase tongue protrusion. Or avoiding exersaucers and jumparoos because they would heighten Penny's hip instability. Or realizing that no clothes were designed to fit her short arms.

In the future I imagined more of the same. Some of it might be scary, but much of it would be normal for us. And if my recent experience with Penny was any indication, the rest of my life as her mother would be filled with delight.

The most natural words to describe her were ones like *cute, sweet, fun, outgoing*. But then the clinical words flitted through my mind: *chromosomal abnormality, mental retardation, disabled.* And the politically correct ones: *special needs, intellectually challenged.* I still didn't know how to describe her in a way that didn't ignore or minimize her extra chromosome but that also didn't define her in entirely negative terms. The words *mental retardation* were helpful in describing the fact that Penny would learn differently, and more slowly, than typical children. But the fact that *retard* and *retarded* had become slurs in our culture eliminated their helpfulness. Then there were the words *disability* and *abnormality.* I thought of those signs on the highway about disabled vehicles. Penny might not be able to do the same things on the same timeline as others, but she was not a "dis-abled" human being, she was not a broken-down, can't-function-until-a-mechanic-comes-along, little girl.

One word I did like was *vulnerable.* Penny was vulnerable—physically, mentally, even socially and emotionally. Another was *dependent.* Penny was, and would be, dependent upon others for some level of care throughout her life. Perhaps the reason I liked those words was because they described what I wanted to admit about myself. That I, too, was vulnerable, much as I liked to see myself as invincible. That I, too, was dependent upon others, much as I liked to think of myself as self-sufficient.

One afternoon, Peter came home from work and held out a piece of paper. "Take a look," he said.

I followed him down the hall to our bedroom and sat on the bed to read. The document was entitled "Proposal for the Moral Education of Lawrenceville Students." As Peter changed out of his jacket and tie, I sat on the bed, scanning the page. When I had finished, I tapped the paper with my index finger. "Okay, she's arguing that because Lawrenceville students have the ability to reason, they have the ability to make moral choices. Right?"

He nodded, emptying his pockets on the bed—keys, a billfold, a Swiss Army knife, three scraps of paper.

"So does that make morality contingent upon intelligence? Poor Penny."

He smiled, as if he had been waiting for that response. "I know. I had the same thought. Especially since I often feel like it's my ability to reason that helps me get out of doing the right thing, like I come up with rationales for bad behavior."

I thought back to arguments Peter and I had early on in our marriage. Often, I had known that he was right about something, but I hadn't wanted to admit it. So I would ask him to provide evidence and make his case, but he wouldn't have any. And then I would go on to defend myself, as if citing chapter and verse, even though my gut would tell me he had it right all along. "I know exactly what you mean. Morality can be governed by intelligence, or it can be thwarted by it. I have to suspect that Penny's moral compass will be just as refined as ours, no matter where her IQ ends up."

Peter nodded and then paused before pulling on a T-shirt. "Sometimes this place seems so restricted. Like we can only understand the world through arguments and data points. But there are other ways to know what's good."

I could hear Penny stirring in her bedroom. As I pushed myself up from the bed, Peter said, "By the way, I want to have Penny baptized."

I had told Peter in the past that I didn't want baptism to come out of a sense of cultural or familial obligation. But just as I didn't believe morality was contingent upon intelligence, I no longer believed knowing God required intellectual assent. As I walked out the door, I met his eyes. "I want her to be baptized, too," I said.

For a long time, infant baptism had seemed too definitive. It seemed to leave out the choice of the child to follow God later in life. It seemed presumptuous. But then I went to seminary, and I realized that following God was not merely a matter of individual will. First and foremost, baptism had to do with God, and with trusting that God, in some mysterious, incalculable way, would bless and lead and care for this child until she reached an age where she could respond to the work of the Spirit in her life. Baptism also had to do with the recognition that Penny wasn't just an individual making a personal decision, but a member of a family and a community who participated in her spiritual formation.

Back in the spring, when Penny was a few months old, an elderly woman came to visit. I held Penny on my lap as this woman described her own daughter, an adult with Down syndrome. "She can't really talk. Intellectually, she's probably like a three-year-old."

I nodded, trying to keep panic from my face.

"She loves church. She loves the music and swaying in her seat. She loves the people. And my sense is that she loves Jesus, even though she's never been able to tell me that." She leaned forward in her seat, as if she might need to whisper her next sentence. "And I let her take Communion, even though I don't know exactly what she believes."

Her daughter couldn't write a treatise or speak a paragraph of explanation about her faith. And yet her daughter had been created in the image of God, with the capacity for relationship with God. As I thought about her swaying in the pews and clapping to the music, it made me wonder whether the intellect even sometimes got in the way of belief rather than being a necessary component of it.

I couldn't reserve baptism for adults who could articulate a profession of faith in Jesus anymore. God was too big for that.

We arranged to use Lawrenceville's chapel for the baptism. On Sunday morning, November 12, we dressed Penny in her great-grandmother's christening gown. She sat on the plush red carpet that surrounded the altar, with her translucent skin and wide blue eyes, her soft brown hair and the long, creamy, lace gown draped around her. The fairy-tale portrait was interrupted by a Boston Red Sox bib, protecting the gown from any drool or food.

"Don't worry," I told my sister Kate, Penny's godmother-to-be. "I'll take it off before the service starts."

Kate leaned down and put her face close to Penny's. "I will make sure your mom remembers to take off the bib."

Penny batted her eyes.

We got everything set up—flowers at the altar, two of Peter's students to hand out programs. I checked in with a friend who had agreed to play the piano. We made sure the microphones worked and that various friends and family members knew their roles in helping the ceremony proceed. As the pews began to fill, I removed Penny's bib and ran my hands along the delicate lace of her gown.

Over one hundred people showed up. Dozens of Peter's colleagues and students. A few friends from church. Family members from all over. Atheists, Jews, Muslims, and Christians all gathered for the occasion. Peter stood to welcome the faces that lined the wooden pews. "I know that sitting in a chapel is not what many of you do every week. But we're so honored that you would choose to be here this morning to join us in receiving God's work in our daughter's life and in our family's life. We've tried to keep the service simple, but we know there will be parts that might feel unfamiliar—prayers or hymns or even the whole baptism thing. Please don't worry if you don't know what's going on, but we hope you'll participate to the degree that you feel comfortable. And be sure to sing out!"

Sing out they did. The voices filled the cavernous space, as if to embrace us. We sang "Praise to the Lord," an old hymn. I had always loved it, but I was struck for the first time by the penultimate verse:

> *Praise to the Lord, Who doth prosper thy way and*
> *defend thee;*
> *Surely His goodness and mercy shall ever attend thee.*

Ponder anew what the Almighty can do, Who with His love doth befriend thee.

Ponder anew what the Almighty can do . . . With Penny propped upon my hip, I thought, *Yes, God can do new things. New things in my life. New things in my heart. New things in our family*. I kissed the top of her head as the hymn came to a close.

A few minutes later, I walked to the lectern to offer my reflections on the readings we had chosen for the day. Kate had read from 1 Corinthians 13, Paul's famous passage about love, most commonly heard at weddings. Our friend Susannah read from Mark 9, where Jesus received the children even though the disciples thought He would see them as a nuisance and had tried to shoo them away. My heart pounded more quickly than usual. I had spoken about my beliefs in a church context before, and in one-on-one conversations, but never to a crowd like this one. And yet the only way for me to explain my love for our daughter was through the lens of faith. I took a deep breath and began:

> The passages that Kate and Susannah just read have meant a lot to us these past ten months. Both of them contain a contrast. In 1 Corinthians 13, Paul begins by talking about things like "speaking in the tongues of men or of angels" or "having faith that can move mountains." He contrasts these things—these impressive traits—with what it means to have love, and he says that without love, those previous things have no value. In the second passage, we hear about Jesus and His disciples, and we receive another contrast. First there are the disciples, wondering who is the greatest. Then there is the child, a representative of "the least

> among them." And it is the child who becomes the model for the disciples, and for all of us.
>
> One week after Penny was born, a friend called and shared that verse from Mark's gospel: "Whoever receives this child, receives me," and she said, "Amy Julia, I have a sense that this is true for you with Penny."
>
> The more we receive Penny, the more we welcome her, exactly as she is, the more we welcome God's work in our lives.

As I spoke, I made eye contact with people in the pews. Some sat with quiet smiles, others were nodding their heads.

> One of the things that Penny's life has shown me so far is how different God's values are from my values, and from many of our culture's values. Going back to Paul's letter to the Corinthians for a minute, I have realized in the past few months that I am very impressed by education, by the ability to be articulate and communicate clearly. I don't think it's bad, in and of itself, for me to be impressed by these things, yet it makes me ask myself whether I am more impressed by good speeches and college degrees than I am by love.

I paused for a moment, scanning the crowd. There was Chris, and Tom, and Michael—Peter's colleagues who each had spent decades in school and still read scholarly journals regularly. There were his students, who all worried about the homework they needed to finish and whether they looked good today and what their future held. There was our family, who knew better than anyone else the truth of my statements.

Kate, who had often urged me to put down the books and play kick-the-can or go for a swim or just hang out. Mom and Dad, who had encouraged me not to work so hard in high school. And here was my chance to say it out loud: I was wrong. For so much of my life I valued the wrong things, or at least I valued them in the wrong way. And this little girl of ours had helped me to see it.

I glanced at Penny, seated on her father's lap in the first pew. Her body swayed, as if she could hear music playing. I kept my eyes on her as I continued:

> It seems to me that God values the love that Paul describes—patient, kind, selfless love—above carefully crafted sentences and even above public professions of faith. I'm pretty sure that Penny is going to teach me a lot about God's values, about God's kind of love.
>
> To give one small example, let me share a story. There was one morning, a few weeks ago, when Penny woke up around five-thirty. I wasn't ready to get out of bed, so I decided to see if she would wait for me. I turned off the monitor, knowing that I would hear her if she cried loudly, and I set the alarm for 6:30. When I woke up an hour later, there was Penny, still quietly babbling in her crib, waiting for me. It struck me then that she might already, as an infant, know more about patient love than I do.
>
> Penny has Down syndrome, an extra twenty-first chromosome in every cell of her body. We were told early on that we could count on two things: that she would have delays in her physical development, and that she would have some degree of cognitive impairment. I'm

starting to realize that, for some reason, her extra chromosome is not only associated with delays and impairments. It is also associated with sweetness, joy, wonder, patience, and love. And despite the challenges her extra chromosome will bring, I wouldn't trade it for the world. Penny is who she is, and we love her more every day.

Today we stand before you all, and before God, delighted to welcome our daughter, Penelope Truesdell Becker, as God's child, God's gift of love to us and, we hope, to this community.

I took my seat, and Daniel, Peter's roommate from college, resumed his place at the front of the chapel. He wore the long black robes that went with his newly acquired seminary degree and his ordination into the Presbyterian Church. He and his wife, Susannah, would become Penny's godparents, along with my sister Kate and Peter's brother Christian. Daniel and Susannah lived in Virginia, but he was still Peter's closest friend. After Penny was born, Daniel was the first person outside of the family whom Peter called.

Daniel offered an explanation of baptism itself, this ancient covenant with God, this symbolic act that mirrored Jesus's death and resurrection. And then he led the congregation in a reminder of the Christian faith: "We believe in God . . ."

They were words I had uttered throughout my life—at Christmas and Easter, every Sunday when Peter and I used to attend an Episcopal church. There were times in my life when they had lost their meaning. There were times when I had wondered if they could possibly be true, these proclamations of faith in a man who was God, in a man who died a criminal's death, in a man whose death was overturned and who offered me life with God forever. And yet that day, in that chapel, with Penny in Peter's arms, the folds of her gown draping down to his knees, I meant every word I spoke. *I believe in a God who doesn't always make sense. I believe in a God who overturns expectations and cannot be controlled by me. I believe in a God who loves so deeply as to be willing to allow us to suffer, that we might know fullness of life.* The words resounded from the pews to the altar, filling the space with faith, with hope. *I believe.*

We proclaimed our faith, and Christian led the congregation in prayer, and then Daniel cupped his hand in the water and poured it over Penny. She squirmed as he said, "We receive you into the household of God. Confess the faith of Christ crucified, proclaim His resurrection, and share with us in His eternal priesthood."

There it was. Our daughter, a daughter in the household of God. One whose life would be marked by God's life. One who would share in Jesus's sufferings and His glory.

Daniel held her in his arms as if she were sitting in a chair and walked her down the aisle as the congregation shared a greeting of peace with one another and reached out to congratulate Penny. We concluded the service with a hymn we had sung at our wedding: "Come Thou Fount of Every Blessing." And like that wedding day seven years earlier, this day was a day of blessing, a day of delight.

It took us a while to get home after the service, but when we did, we finally opened the bottle of champagne that had remained corked in the hospital after Penny's arrival. Surrounded by family and friends, we raised our glasses to welcome our daughter.

PART THREE

just penny

Penny found herself in the mirror yesterday, and she is in love! She continues to surprise us with how healthy and fun and wonderful she is. It is as if this monster called Down syndrome has been tamed into a house pet. When we notice her low muscle tone or think about the little hole in her heart, those are the moments when we remember that she has an extra chromosome. But most of the time she's just a delightful little girl who learns new things every day. Lately, the new things have been feeding herself Cheerios, crackers, and muenster cheese (her very favorite food); bending over and reaching for her rattle; passing toys from one hand to another; raising her arms over her head when she wants to be picked up; kissing my cheek with gusto (open mouth, lots of slobber, and an affectionate "aaahhh"); and babbling with so many different intonations, we think she's trying to sing. As the last sentence might indicate, we are also in love, and we're very proud of our little girl.

November 2006

14

Over the course of the year since Penny was born, I found myself less and less beholden to books and charts that told me when she should accomplish various cognitive or physical milestones. Back in the spring, when she was only two months old, Peter and I had attended a conference where we heard a child development specialist speak about "responsive parenting." He said most parents of kids with disabilities focused on their child's weaknesses. Instead we should try to identify Penny's strengths and help her grow into those strengths. That way she would maintain interest and enjoyment as she played, and we would recognize how capable she really was. Ideally, the process would begin a happy feedback loop, where progress was made not because of fighting to get to the next goal, but because of getting to know our daughter as an individual who could do things in her way, in her time.

Up until we heard that man's lecture, I had a sense of urgency about Penny's care. *If only we find the right doctor . . . if only I am faithful to do infant massage, baby yoga . . . if only we identify the right foods and nutritional supplements and therapists and . . .* But his words helped me realize that Penny wasn't a problem to be fixed. She was our daughter, a person to be loved.

From then on I tried to disregard the lists of developmental expectations and instead focus upon getting to know her. I resisted when the therapists asked me to set a goal for our next meeting. "I just want to help her achieve the next thing," I said. "Whatever that is." And she did. She took her time, but she achieved the next thing. Smiling. Reaching. Sitting up. Rolling. Responding to our words. Babbling on her own. It was as if I started off with my fist clenched tight around a vision of a child and, as Penny grew, I slowly opened my fingers. The bits and pieces of my fictional daughter scattered in the wind, and I was left with an open palm.

But once my palm was open, Penny started to surprise me. One night in November, with Peter away at a conference, I was giving her a bath. She sat, as usual, like a queen in court. I poured water over her head and lathered her hair. The phone rang. It was Peter.

"Hi there," I said. "I'm just giving Penny a bath."

"I was calling to tell her good-night. I can call back."

"That's okay. Let's see what she does."

I held the phone near Penny's face. She inspected it for a moment, this foreign object with noises coming out of the receiver. I could hear Peter's voice, "Hi, Penny. Hello, Penny." He kept talking, and she continued to stare at the source of his monologue.

And then she cocked her head and turned her face to me. "Dadadada?"

There was a flutter in my sternum as I said, "Yes, sweetie. Dada is on the phone. He's calling to say good-night."

She looked very pleased with herself.

"You're not supposed to know that," I murmured.

She smiled and splashed the water.

Now that Penny was almost one year old, we reported to the Children's Hospital of Philadelphia again, this time for an appointment with Dr. Post, a developmental pediatrician who worked exclusively with children with Down syndrome. Our visit began with evaluations. First, an occupational therapist. She watched Penny manipulate blocks, pull strings, shake rattles, and generally examine any number of toys sent her way. I craned my neck to glimpse the therapist's clipboard with its measurements of Penny's progress. She tallied it up, nodding her head as she went. At the end of half an hour of playing and ten minutes of scoring, the therapist bit her lip for just a moment before looking me in the eye. "The scale we use gives us a comparison between Penny and other kids her age."

I nodded, casting a sidelong glance at Peter.

"And I think you should be really encouraged by all the things Penny's doing."

"We are," Peter said. He leaned forward in his chair, spinning his wedding band on his ring finger.

Then, sounding apologetic, she said, "Penny is in the twelfth percentile compared to other children her age."

"The twelfth? Compared to typical kids?" I thought back to our regular checkups at the pediatrician's office, where Dr. Bill hesitated to show me Penny's growth on the charts he used with everyone else. Even on the chart specific to kids with Down syndrome, she only measured in the tenth percentile. When it came to the regular charts, she didn't register at all. So when this therapist told me, as if it were bad news, that Penny's fine motor skills were delayed, I didn't register her disappointment. "You mean Penny is on the chart? Wow."

I looked at Peter straight on this time, noting the pleased expression on his face. His hands were quiet now.

She smiled. "Your daughter is doing great."

There it was again, that flutter in my chest. It was as if I had given up on any thought that Penny might excel in some areas. I didn't want my love for her to be linked to her achievements. I didn't want to get caught up in comparisons. I didn't want to set myself, or her, up for disappointment. But I did want to believe in her.

"She's a lovely little girl," the therapist said. She tore off a carbon copy of the scores and handed them to me.

From there, we wheeled Penny's stroller across the hall to meet with a physical therapist.

"She's been sitting up since seven months, but she hasn't seemed very interested in doing anything else," Peter told her.

"I have a son with Down syndrome," the therapist replied. "They do things in their own time. I'll just try to give you a sense of when that time might be for Penny."

Peter and I described Penny's progress. That she had started to roll and then stopped. That she hated tummy time. That she did have a physical therapist but she tired easily. Throughout our description, Penny sat. She craned her neck to take in her surroundings, never wavering from that firm spot on the floor. The therapist tried to motivate Penny to reach for a toy and topple onto the mat. Penny moved a few inches and then snapped back to attention. The therapist said, "You know, it may be another year before Penny is crawling."

Gulp. Heart pounding. Eyes closed for a moment. *She's doing great.*

"What's the next thing she needs to learn?" Peter asked.

"Well, she needs to be willing to lose her balance," the therapist said. "See." She pulled Penny's hands to the side, forcing one hip off the floor. "She's so proud of herself for sitting up that she doesn't want to risk leaning over. It's not really that she can't do it. Just that she won't."

I thought of myself in yoga class. Our teacher always talked about strength, flexibility, and balance. I had adequate strength. My body had never been particularly flexible. But balance. There I excelled. I could sway with my hands overhead in tree pose—one leg straight, the other propped on the inner thigh—for longer than anyone else in the class. Put me in dancer—one leg extended behind me and grasped with my hand. It might not look pretty, but I didn't wobble. The same was true in my life. A change in plans, a spontaneous outing, a friend who popped in to say hi during Penny's nap—even happy interruptions often made me grumble. But making sure I got enough sleep and worked when I said I would work and kept my daughter on a schedule and ate dinner at the same time every night—a healthy work/family/life balance came naturally. At least in the gross motor skills department, Penny was just like me.

"You know," the therapist said a few minutes later, as she gently and repeatedly pushed Penny off her bottom and onto the floor. "I think this baby wants to move, and I think she may even be crawling within the next six months."

I pulled my hand to my mouth, as if to hide the thought that was making me smile. Penny just needed to get comfortable with losing her balance.

Our last stop was with Dr. Post herself. We had waited months for this appointment, and I felt a strange sense of anticipation, as if Dr. Post were a celebrity deigning to offer me an autograph.

She was all business. She had a briefcase of plastic tools and a scoring system and a brusque clinical demeanor. But her eyes were kind, with crinkles that told me she laughed a lot, at least when she wasn't in the office. A scribe took notes as we narrated Penny's development to that point, and then Dr. Post turned to our daughter.

"Penny, what do you do when I say 'up'?" Penny raised her hands. Dr. Post pulled out a mirror and watched Penny gaze at herself. She dropped a block and observed Penny's eyes. She put the block in front of Penny. She put two blocks in front. She asked us questions, checking boxes and nodding.

"Well," she said, leaning back in her rolling chair once she'd finished the assessment. "You may have heard that children with Down syndrome are at an increased risk for autism."

Peter's eyes grew wide. I nodded and recited what I remembered from reading statistics early on in Penny's life: "Ten percent of kids with Down syndrome have autism."

"She's young, but I just want you to know that your daughter does not fall anywhere on the autism spectrum. Her communication skills are close to age-appropriate. But she's not going to be able to talk for a while even though she wants to communicate. I highly recommend sign language until she's ready to speak her words."

"Okay," I nodded, making a note of it. "Is there anything you're concerned about?"

"Well, she's lagging as far as gross motor, but that will come with time. She just needs to increase her strength. I'll send you a full report with my recommendations, but all told, you really have nothing to worry about. You're welcome to return for another visit next fall, but it won't be necessary, as long as you're able to get the proper supports in place."

When we left, the flutter in my chest seemed permanent. I had thrown away my comparisons to baby books that told me what Penny ought to be able to do. I wasn't about to go back. But now I was starting to discard the ideas I had of what she shouldn't be able to do. It threw me off balance, this inability to plan for her future. But it was fun, too. A bit like toppling over and finding a big mat filled with toys right in front of me.

A week later, we boarded a plane for my family's annual vacation. I had memories from years past of lying on the beach and reading novel after novel, laughing with my sisters, gathering for a cocktail to watch the sunset, cooking dinner together, and staying up late playing games or just talking.

I wondered if Penny's presence would feel like a burden—nursing, naps, the constant mess of learning to eat solid food. But instead she brought laughter wherever she went. In the morning, banging pots and pans on the floor as Mom puttered about and Peter and I tried to get more sleep. Throughout the day, sitting in her high chair smearing food on the tray in front of her, with Aunt Elly's cowboy hat drooped over her head. In the evening, leaning in for a kiss that covered her Uncle Frank's cheek in drool.

That week Penny started to call me "Baba." She started waving whenever a family member walked into view. She stuffed handfuls of sand into her mouth and crinkled her nose.

One afternoon I was sitting by the pool. Kate lay on her stomach on a lounge chair nearby. I stationed Penny in front of me and said, "Kate, look! She's standing!" What I really meant was that she was bearing a little weight on her legs for the first time.

Kate rolled over and propped herself up to see Penny. She clapped as Penny's knees buckled. A smile spread across Penny's face. She was dressed in a hot pink suit with a ruffle and a flower, and she sat down with an emphatic thump, bouncing a few times on the mesh of the lounge chair.

"You know," Kate said, "sometimes I think Penny's life is more significant than any of the rest of ours."

I could feel my forehead wrinkle. "What do you mean?" I thought about our family. Dad was a successful businessman. Mom taught preschool and had raised the four of us while Dad worked. Kate and her husband, Frank, both ran successful small businesses. Brooks had only recently graduated from college, but she had a job as an events planner and a steady boyfriend. Elly was getting good grades and was social chair of her sorority at UVa. All of them were considered nice people. Everyone had a significant life by any measure I'd ever used.

Kate pushed herself up from her chair. "Well, the fact that Penny has an extra chromosome makes her unusual. And I know some people see that as a negative, but I see it as a positive. It sets her apart. She's so similar to us that we can understand her, but, I don't know, it's like even though she has to work harder, she has this amazing attitude. It just makes me think she has more to offer."

I found myself nodding, even though I wasn't totally sure I understood, or totally sure I agreed. "But you knew more about Down syndrome than I did when Penny was born, and you cried and cried and cried." I had always wondered about Kate's response to Penny's birth. It had scared me—that my sister who treasured her friendship with her Best Buddy, Mandy, had nonetheless wept when her niece was born with the same condition.

"I wasn't crying for Penny, I don't think," she said. "I was crying because I've seen how hard it can be—that people make fun of people with Down syndrome, or stare at a family walking into a restaurant. Or when I went back to work the day after she was born and saw all my kids in class and thought of Penny struggling to be friends with them or to do ballet . . . You're right. I cried all day. But it wasn't because of Penny. It was because of the rest of us." She took off her sunglasses and ran her index finger under her eyes, giving me a quick smile. "Want to go for a swim, my love?" she asked her niece.

And soon they were in the pool, with Kate singing, "Puh-puh-puh Penny, beautiful Penny, you're the only little girl that I adore . . ." as I pondered her words.

We went to a local hotel's restaurant for Thanksgiving dinner. Being in such a public place made me remember all those comments that had come throughout my life, especially on vacation, about our "perfect family." Here we were, strolling around a resort with a baby with Down syndrome. Most people didn't seem to notice. There was a steel drum band playing, and Peter took Penny close so she could bounce and sway to the music. He held her in his arms and twirled around, her eyes wide with delight.

During a break, the band leader approached Peter and Penny. He squatted down so he could look Penny in the eye. After a long pause, he turned to Peter. "She's beautiful," he said. "She has an old soul."

A few days later we returned to Lawrenceville. Eliza, one of the girls from Bible study, stopped by for a visit. Penny sat on the floor, clapping, bouncing, waving, and every so often doing her newest cute trick, which was to bring both hands to the sides of her face with a coy smile.

I shook my head at this little girl, with her sparkling eyes and round cheeks and perpetual smile. "I never could have imagined that my daughter with Down syndrome would be like this."

And Eliza responded, "She's not really your daughter with Down syndrome. She's just Penny."

I felt a wave of recognition wash over me, as if my heart had been waiting to hear the truth of her statement.

It had taken us nearly a year, but we finally figured it out. She wasn't a mistake. She wasn't a Down syndrome baby. To us, she was no longer even our-daughter-with-Down-syndrome. She was just Penny.

I am filled with contradictory emotions: "The hopes and fears of all the years are met in thee tonight." Struck by how much hope I have for Penny—that she will live a full life with friends and laughter and arguments with her siblings and an ability to give back to her community and a knowledge of God's love. Hope that she will go to public school and that her heart will heal and that she will speak clearly and read and write and walk and run and dance. Hope that she will sing and play music and ride horses. Hope that she will be received by many for who she is, valued by many, loved. Hope that she will surpass expectations—physical, mental, social, emotional. So much hope.

And with that hope comes intense fear that little of it will come to pass, that she will suffer, be mocked, that her little body will betray her. Fear that she won't succeed, or that she won't have friends, or that we won't be able to give her what she needs. Fear that Down syndrome is what I thought it was a year ago. Fear that our culture is right, that she is undesirable, that an extra chromosome is a mistake. I don't want to hope, sometimes, because I don't want the fear that accompanies the hope.

December 2006

15

I hugged my arms across my chest. It was a clear night—cold, no wind, two days before Christmas. We had left Penny at my parents' house with a baby-sitter, and Peter and I were walking through a local park on our way to meet my family for dinner in town. I took in the silhouettes of weeping willows, the duck pond, the outline of a picturesque wooden bridge. The water was black, with hints of ice on its surface. I glanced at Peter.

"I think I had a miscarriage last month."

He nodded, and his face looked rigid, whether from my statement or from the cold, I couldn't tell.

Five weeks earlier, I had taken a pregnancy test. I had been about to throw it away when I noticed a faint blue line. I woke Peter up. "There's something I need you to take a look at," I said. And there it was, this tiny acknowledgment of life within my body, of another member of our family. The baby would have been about three weeks old, a clump of cells, with the material in place for a heart and skeleton and brain and skin and all the other organs. After I told him, we had prayed together, kneeling on the floor with Penny babbling on the bed in front of us.

Later that same day, I had started to bleed. I told Peter that the test had been wrong. I insisted to myself that I hadn't really been pregnant, even though I was a week late, even though the bleeding was heavy, even though I knew it was near impossible to have a false positive. But once December came, and I went through another monthly cycle, I couldn't deny the physical facts anymore. It had been a miscarriage. Early, very early, but a miscarriage nonetheless.

We walked on, my arm linked in his. The cold stung my cheeks.

"How are you?" Peter asked. Though I didn't look at him, I could hear the concern in his voice.

"I'm okay." My reply was immediate, as if I didn't want to think about my answer, as if I wanted to take the pond's thin layer of ice into myself. "I can't say I'm sad. There wasn't enough time to start thinking of it as a baby, really. It's just . . . Well, I guess I just need to call Dr. Mayer."

Something similar had happened when Penny was five months old. After some unexplained bleeding, Dr. Mayer had asked me to take a pregnancy test and it had come back positive. An hour later, I took another test, and it turned out negative. I wasn't pregnant. Dr. Mayer had called it a "chemical pregnancy." I hadn't thought too much of it. I hadn't wanted to be pregnant, and I figured the test had just been wrong. But now I was starting to think I had miscarried twice in six months.

"I'm really scared," I said.

Peter reached out and touched my shoulder until I slowed my pace. He held me for a moment, just long enough to slow my thoughts. My shoulders shuddered.

"I never thought this would be us," I said.

"I know," Peter replied.

What else could he say?

On Christmas Eve we drove to my grandparents' home, a rambling Victorian house in a classic New England town. My grandfather greeted us at the back door. He put his face close to Penny and said, "Well hello, beautiful!" She laughed.

Grampa stood up straight to give us both a hug. Penny responded by sticking out her tongue, puffing her cheeks full of air, and spitting in his face.

Eyebrows raised, Grampa said, "Why Penelope, my dear, tell me how you really feel!"

We joined a host of cousins and aunts and uncles in the living room. A fire crackled in the fireplace and Handel's *Messiah* played in the background. Everyone wanted to see Penny in her red velvet dress with white trim and matching hat, spitting and kissing and giggling with anyone who came her way. I took her in my arms to give her a tour of the house. "See, Penny, this is your mama when she was a baby. . . . And this is a painting of your great-great-great-great-grandfather, who lived in this town a long time ago. . . . And these are the carolers your Nana made. . . ." I pointed to a row of figures. Eleven in all—the four sisters and our seven cousins, each with an identifying prop. This year Penny would be added to the lineup.

"It's a very special family," I told her.

She wriggled in my arms.

We soon headed down the street to church for the annual Christmas pageant and took our customary seats in the balcony. As Penny grew restless, Peter leaned over. "I'll take her out for a while."

I turned my attention back to the scene unfolding before me, the reenactment of what had happened all those years ago, the people streaming to visit the baby in the manger, the angels making pronouncements about the meaning of His life. I remembered from my theology classes that many of the early Christians hadn't emphasized Jesus's death on the cross or resurrection from the dead as the events that saved the world. They had focused instead on His birth, the incarnation.

We stood to sing "O Little Town of Bethlehem." The tune was familiar, but I hadn't ever paid attention to the words before. *The hopes and fears of all the years are met in thee tonight.*

So much depended upon this birth, this life, this child. In the very act of becoming a baby, God was overcoming everything that divided humanity from the heavenly realm. God had opened the chasm and bridged the gap simply by entering into human flesh, into our world.

Gregory of Nazianzus, an early bishop, had said, "That which God has not assumed, God cannot redeem." We couldn't be saved by a human being, he reasoned. But neither could we be saved by God unless God saved us entirely, by becoming one of us. I had appreciated his point when I first came across it. But now, looking at that baby doll representing Jesus, I had to wonder what His birth meant for Penny. What would it mean for Jesus to have redeemed us all, including the ones with an extra chromosome? Could Jesus have come as a baby with Down syndrome? And what about the miscarriage? Had Jesus redeemed that tiny clump of cells that had never been born?

Penny remained festive throughout Christmas and into her first birthday. She enjoyed the wrapping paper in equal measure to the laughter of adoring relatives and paid little attention to her pile of gifts. When we sang "Happy Birthday," she signaled her unqualified approval by shouting with delight from start to finish. And yet, throughout the celebrations, I felt myself pulling back. With the miscarriage still on my mind, I cradled fear and doubt, as attentive to their pull as I would have been to a newborn.

Three days after Penny's birthday, I flew to South Carolina. My seminary scholarship required that I join other recipients for an annual retreat, a time to share the struggles and blessings of theological training as we prayed and learned together.

There was something almost intoxicating about the promise of time to think and sleep and read and be by myself. And yet worshiping God was the last thing I wanted. My faith was perched on the edge of a cliff, in danger of toppling into oblivion if even a small storm came along. I had so many doubts, so many fears, including the fear that other Christians would judge me for all my questions. I knew the standard line, but I wasn't satisfied with theological explanations for the pain I had witnessed when taking Penny for checkups at the hospital over the past year. What could ever redeem the suffering of all those little ones? I stepped off that plane with an open wound in my soul, a wound that had been festering without my knowledge all these months, a wound that had been ripped open with this most recent loss.

The architecture of the retreat center was simple, and it made for a somewhat bleak first impression—buildings of inexpensive brick that sat low to the ground, floors of linoleum or industrial carpet. Yet something about its simplicity brought a sense of peace. Outside, the trees were bare and the grass brown. But even though it was January, the air held a suggestion of warmth, of green buds and dandelions and robins' eggs.

I unpacked my clothes and stacked a few books on the bedside table. I picked up my journal and opened it, only to find a series of empty pages. I kept a separate journal with my thoughts about Penny; this one was meant to be a place for prayer requests and thoughts about God. It had hardly gotten any use since I had bought it four months before.

"Well, here's your chance," I said out loud. With less confidence, and I'm not sure if it was a thought or a prayer, I said, "I believe. Help my unbelief." And then I squared my shoulders and walked out the door.

On my way to dinner, I bumped into a fellow seminarian, a young woman who had participated in the retreat two years earlier. We traded hugs and started an easy stream of chitchat.

"How's your daughter? Don't you miss her so much?" she asked.

I laughed. "You know what? I don't. I mean, I'm sure I will soon enough, but right now it's just nice to be here. My mom and Peter are with Penny, so she's in very good hands."

As we opened the door to the dining hall, she said, "So how does it feel to be a Down's parent?"

Her words were earnest, interested, laid before me as casually as possible, and yet the question changed the tone. I said, "I actually think of it as being a parent of a child who has Down syndrome."

She didn't have time to respond. Our group was already assembled in a semicircle. We took our places, and I stood shoulder to shoulder with my friend, although I felt the temptation to take a step back. To take the place I felt I had been assigned, in a separate category of parent with a separate category of child.

There were about twenty of us alongside the men who lived at the monastery. One of the brothers stood up to pray and read Scripture before our meal. He walked to the podium with an awkward gait, as if his hips and legs were hewn of the same piece. His head tilted slightly to the side. He opened the Bible and began to page through. Back and forth, back and forth.

People around me began to shift their weight. Impatience rose like steam from a boiling pot of water, wispy at first, and then picking up in speed and intensity. I held my breath, willing him to speak.

He looked up. Another brother walked to his side, and the reader said, "I can't find the passage." His words were somewhat unclear, as if he had rocks in his mouth.

The younger brother located the passage and stepped back, and the first man proclaimed, "In the beginning, God created the heavens and the earth." He finished reading Genesis 1, offered a blessing for our meal, and turned to get in line for food.

As we moved to pick up trays and utensils for dinner, greeting other friends and maintaining steady conversation about our lives, I kept thinking about the brother behind the podium. Had I watched the same scene unfold a year earlier, I would have been annoyed by the delay, maybe even embarrassed by his predicament. I could imagine the questions that would have been running through my head—*Why can't they find someone who can read, who at least knows where the first book in the Bible is located?* But today, I could have listened to him for an hour. Without knowing it, he had welcomed me, with his imperfect speech and the fact that he needed help finding Genesis. He allowed me to envision Penny one day reading the Bible in public. He allowed me to believe Penny could be treated as a fellow child of God without distinction, without dividing lines.

That night I picked up the journal. I wrote,

> *The words that keep running through my heart are safety and protection. I am afraid that God will not keep us safe. And I wonder if these are words that expose my fear of the Lord. Is this a reverent fear? Or the fear of the wicked servant in Jesus' parable who doesn't really understand the character of God? I hope it is the fear that the writer of Proverbs references—the fear of the Lord that is the beginning of wisdom. Because I know that faith in God—full assent to God—means faith in God's goodness come what may, faith in God's faithfulness even when confused, knowledge that God is not content to let me stay the way I am, but that God will insist upon changing me, whatever it takes.*

Two nights later, our whole group convened for dinner. We numbered forty or fifty people in all—two dozen seminary students, the retreat speakers, and a dozen more local sponsors of our scholarship. It was a fun evening by seminary standards—good food and wine, conversation about theology. The hosts had even hired a magician. He worked the crowd, pulling a large silver coin from behind my ear and then making it vanish only to appear again in my friend's purse. Some members of our group shadowed him all evening, intent on discovering his secrets. I was content to suspend disbelief. After dinner, the magician took his leave and we gathered in the living room where the couple who had founded the scholarship, Leighton and Jeanie Ford, gave us a chance to ask questions.

They were in their seventies—his hair white, hers salt-and-peppered. They had established the scholarship decades earlier after their son Sandy died when he was in college, before he could fulfill his own dreams of attending seminary.

The questions were winding down, and I raised my hand. Jeanie looked at me and nodded.

I said, "You talked tonight about the purpose God had through this scholarship, and yet I'm struck by the fact that the scholarship wouldn't have started if it hadn't been for a tragedy in your life. And I'm wondering how you think about Sandy's death now." I wanted to know how they had lived with it, with the everyday knowledge that they were alive and their son was not, with the everyday sadness that his life was not what they had expected it to be.

Jeanie stroked the arm of the chair as if it were a cat, with absent-minded gentleness. "For all my gratitude for all of you," she said, moving her head to acknowledge the whole room, "and for all my gratitude for the hundreds of other students who came before you, for the twenty-five years that we've had scholarships and fellowship with all of you . . ." Her hand stopped moving. "I would trade it all in. I would trade it all in for the chance to run my fingers through Sandy's gray hair."

The last sentence she spoke to me, her eyes fixed on my face.

And as my eyes filled up with tears, I nodded. She knew what I was really asking. Even though she could see purpose in her son's death, even though hundreds of young men and women had gone on to become pastors and teachers and serve the world through this scholarship, with all that, it wasn't enough. It would never explain Sandy's absence. It would never make up for her loss.

My story was different, and yet her words acted as a balm. They gave me permission to keep asking questions and move forward in faith at the same time. The thing was, I could see God's hand, God's work, God's care in Penny's life. Starting with the Spirit's voice, "But then you wouldn't have had *this* child." Thinking of the joy and light that Penny gave to us and to so many others. Peter's insistence that she could talk to angels. The way her life had smashed idols in my heart and begun to teach me of love. The way I was able to see other people now.

And yet there was this pervasive sadness in me, this resistance, this voice that cried out *no*. I knew that we were privileged to have her, but it seemed our privilege came at her expense. She was the one with the body that was vulnerable and limited. She was the one with the shorter life expectancy, the one who might never live independently, who probably wouldn't have children of her own.

How could I hold these things together, the gratitude and the loss? The hope and the fear?

The next morning we were invited to walk through a labyrinth, a circuitous path etched in stone in the center of a small garden. Our leader instructed, "As you walk, consider praying the words, *Lord, I trust you.*"

I set out along the curving path, stopping every so often, praying those words, *Lord, I trust you. Lord, I trust you. I trust you with my family. I trust you with my career. I trust you with Penny.* But it wasn't true. They were empty words, prayed out of obedience. And on the heels of that thought came the realization that I wasn't sure that God was trustworthy. I was still walking slowly, but now my fists were clenched and it was as if I were alone, in court, pacing before a judge, demanding that God answer me. *How can I trust you to protect us? How can I trust that you will take care of Penny? After two miscarriages, how can I trust that you will care for our family? After seeing all those children in the hospital—in wheelchairs and on feeding tubes and stretchers—how can I trust you? How can I ever again find the faith to trust you?*

I reached the center of the labyrinth, a circle, and I stood there, head down. No words came. I waited, but there was nothing, just an emptiness, like a room that had been cleared of furniture, with bits of paper fluttering around.

I walked out slowly, silent.

I found a bench nearby and pulled out my Bible. I held it in my hand unopened, as if I were weighing the risk of turning the pages. I thought back to the magician the night before, the card tricks and coins that showed up in places they couldn't have been, with a wave of a wand, with sleight of hand and optical illusion. I knew I shouldn't treat the Bible that way, like a Magic 8 Ball that would cater its words to my questions. The Word of God was serious business, telling a story that spanned generations. It wasn't to be manipulated.

And yet I didn't know what else to do but hope that God would speak to me. I opened the Bible at random to Psalm 116. It began,

> *I love the Lord, for he heard my voice; he heard my cry for mercy.*

I read on, and every word seemed to be written for me, to me. And then I reached verse 6:

> *The Lord protects the simplehearted; when I was in great need, he saved me.*
> *Be at rest once more, O my soul, for the Lord has been good to you.*

It came as a promise. *I have been good to you. I will protect your family. Your daughter will be protected from harm. Your soul can heal. Your soul can rest.*

That week, we'd had an ongoing conversation about the nature of prayer. I was struck by how often my prayer life resembled a grocery list. Share the things I need and then tick them off the list one at a time. Without really expecting an answer. Without listening for God's response. Without faith that prayer matters, that it really can change things, that it actually allows us to know God more fully.

A number of my classmates had felt the same way, and so we had decided to come together with the expectation that God would be with us as we prayed, leading us in prayer, hearing us and answering.

We gathered that afternoon. At first, I sat on the edge of a wing chair, elbows on my knees, eyes closed. A few people were standing, others seated on the couch. In my mind I saw a picture of Mary of Bethany kneeling before Jesus, having let go of her tasks and worries as she simply sat at His feet and learned. I slid from the chair onto the floor.

Someone asked if I wanted prayer, and I nodded. I could feel strong, warm hands on my shoulder, my back, the top of my head.

Our leader prayed out loud, "Spirit, if you have anything to say, speak through us."

The first word I heard was from Tom. "Release," he said.

And then another voice, "Lay it down."

I was so disappointed. I had tried and tried and tried, and those commands were exactly the things I was unable to do. I couldn't release all the fear and doubt and worry. I couldn't lay it down. I wanted to stand up and walk away.

But then Mark prayed, "Lord, I remember reading an essay Amy Julia wrote a few years back. And I remember that she wrote about your promise to be with us. Not your promise to take away pain or to explain everything, but your promise to be present in the midst of our pain and in the midst of our questions. So be with her now, Lord. Be with her. Release her. Lay it down for her."

His words spilled over me like a warm rain.

And another friend spoke up. "When I see Amy Julia kneeling here, what comes to mind is Mary of Bethany sitting before Jesus and receiving from Him. I see her doing what Jesus says is the best thing."

I flew home that evening. Penny was asleep when I arrived, arms and legs splayed, facial muscles relaxed. I reached over the side of the crib to rest my hand on hers. I hadn't received any clear answers to the questions I was asking. No new explanations for pain in the world. No promises that my life would be easier from now on. Just a reminder that God was with us, through a baby in a manger, through suffering, through a cross. Through a child with Down syndrome, in the midst of a miscarriage, in the midst of worry and grief and doubt. As I watched Penny's chest rise and fall, there was peace.

Be at rest once more, O my soul, for the Lord has been good to you.

Penny has started clapping and waving. She raises her hands over her head when I say, "How big is Penny?" and she lets go of her spoon when I ask. I always say, "Good girl," and she claps for herself. She is beginning to pivot and scoot and slowly, cautiously, move around.

I still get overwhelmed by the breadth of the difficulties she could face with this extra chromosome. The little things—thin hair, creased palms, widely spaced toes . . . The physiology—soft spots, small ears and nose, misshapen teeth, hearing loss, poor eyesight, speech problems, large tongue, small mouth, low muscle tone, heart defects, lung vulnerabilities.

The deck is so stacked against her, and yet she is thriving. What a gift.

January 2007

16

I stepped out of the shadows of Penny's bedroom. Peter was waiting for me in the hallway, and he opened his arms for a long hug. From there, we got ready for bed, but then we lay awake for a long time as I shared the details of my week. We had talked on the phone while I was away, but only in person could I try to convey my renewed sense of peace and hope and gratitude. The new faith that God cared about me, about us. That even in my anger and doubt, God would respond. That I didn't need answers as much as I needed love.

After he heard my account—the tears, the prayers, the repeated image of sitting at Jesus's feet—he asked, "Did you miss Penny?"

"I was glad to see her when I got home," I said. "But no, I didn't really miss her. Is that terrible? It was as if I needed to be away from her in order to sort through some of this stuff. I did miss you."

"Age," he said, "I worry sometimes, because this has been so much harder for you."

I cocked my head, waiting for more.

"It was hard for me when Penny was born. Those first twenty-four hours were the darkest ones of my life. But since then, I've been pretty much fine." He shrugged. "And sometimes I worry that my lack of doubt and anger has been hard for you. That somehow you might feel judged by me or something. But I think how you've been feeling totally makes sense, even though I haven't felt the same way."

I pictured Peter and Penny together—when he scooped her into his arms and turned on jazz from New Orleans and danced, when he threw her in the air to bring on giggles, when he helped her work through the motions from sitting to standing up, all the while whispering encouraging words. I shook my head. "I can see why you might think I felt judged. But you haven't made me feel that way at all. It's funny. Your attitude has actually been a gift to me. I watch you with her and listen to you talk about her, and it's just this unadulterated love. It's exactly what I want you to feel. It's exactly what I want to feel, even though for me it gets complicated by all my doubts and fears. The way I see it is that you've let me wander off wherever I need to go, but you've given me a place to return."

I pivoted so I could lean against him, feel the rhythm of his chest, his arms across my body, holding me together, keeping me safe. "Thank you," I said.

The following weekend, we packed the car for a few days with Peter's college roommates. He had lived with ten other guys for his junior and senior years, and they still kept in touch and got together on an annual basis. Over time the reunion grew to include wives and children, and this year we were all convening in a rental house on the Maryland Shore.

Our family arrived after dinner. Penny had fallen asleep in the car, so we whispered greetings to our friends and put her straight to bed. When we emerged, Peter joined his old roommates for a game of spades, and I accepted a cup of tea from Susannah and curled up in a chair near the other women.

I had seen Susannah at Penny's baptism two months earlier, but it had been nearly a year since the rest of us had been together. There were two new babies and another on the way. The conversation took a natural turn and one of the other wives asked me, "So, do ya'll hope to have more kids?" It was an inevitable question, but I wasn't prepared.

"We do. How about you?"

I didn't really listen to her answer or to the reflections on pregnancy and childbirth from the other moms lounging nearby. I just kept thinking about Dr. Mayer's concerns. My appointment to discuss the miscarriage had come earlier that week. Dr. Mayer wondered out loud whether every time Peter and I conceived we passed along a chromosomal abnormality. She wanted to perform tests on both of us. She had said to me, "You deserve a typical child." I winced a little at the memory. I didn't deserve the child I already had. And people who couldn't conceive weren't undeserving. I needed to be open to the possibility that I couldn't get pregnant again, or that I would get pregnant with another child with Down syndrome, or that we needed to consider adoption, or that Penny would be an only child.

And yet I wanted a brother or sister for Penny. And I wanted her for them. All I could do was hold out that hope, and wait.

I looked around the room at all the other young mothers, feeling a seed of resentment take root inside me. I knew I wasn't being fair—the year before, two of these same women had shared stories of miscarriages of their own. And another, who wasn't present that night, had talked about her struggle with infertility. But I couldn't wrench myself from the sense that mine was the precarious position, the lonely road. I feigned a yawn and headed to bed.

In the morning, Penny and I let Peter sleep while we joined the other mothers and children in the kitchen. I plopped Penny onto the floor. Of the four other children, two were her age, and two were six months younger. I told myself not to make comparisons, but as I watched Ellen Grace, just a few days older than Penny, run from one side of the room to the other, I couldn't contain the feeling of being on an elevator that had lost its connection. I was plummeting down, and there was no way to stop the descent.

Earlier that week, we had sat with Penny's social worker and Missy, her therapist, to revise her Individualized Family Service Plan, her "IFSP." Penny had reached her first birthday, so it was time for another evaluation. Missy concluded that Penny's gross motor skills were at a seven-month level. She scored Penny's cognitive, communication, and social/emotional skills at ten months, her fine motor at eleven, self-help at fourteen. Missy was specifically trained as a physical therapist, and she would continue to work with Penny once a week. But now she recommended other specialists—speech therapy twice a month, occupational therapy twice a month, possibly a special educator within the next year. I tried to take it all as an encouragement. There was a state-funded system that supported our daughter's development. I was able to learn from these professionals in our own home with one-on-one instruction. But all my positive thoughts faded in the wake of one-year-olds toddling around the room while Penny sat still, unable even to move herself into a standing position.

I turned my attention to the younger ones. I noticed the strength in their bodies, as if their muscles knew how to hold them upright intuitively, whereas Penny's had to be taught what to do to navigate the world. But when I waved to little Simon, he didn't acknowledge me. Penny, on the other hand, responded to my gesture with a wave, a clap, hands up over her head, and then waving again with two hands at once.

She brought a smile to my face, but I couldn't stop evaluating. All day I calculated how long it would be until Penny could climb on the couch like the other kids, how long it would be before the younger ones surpassed her.

I went to bed that night with a sense of defeat. I had never spent a day with other kids who were so close to Penny in age, and I had never succumbed so fully to the temptation to compare. I thought back to an email that had been forwarded to me a few days earlier. It contrasted "spectrum moms"

(moms with children on the autism spectrum) and "soccer moms." It talked about all the noble things we moms of kids with disabilities did: driving to multiple therapists and negotiating school options and figuring out food and exercise and learning for our kids. It was a nice reminder that I wasn't alone, that there were plenty of other parents working out the same issues on behalf of their children. It even reminded me that plenty of parents and children face far more difficult challenges than I did every day. I was uneasy, though, with the tone, a tone I knew I took on when comparing myself with my friends—that same tone of proud self-pity that had hovered over me all day. When I read that email, it made me think how grateful I was that Early Intervention and the Americans with Disabilities Act and Individualized Family Service Plans existed. How thankful I was that Penny could come with us this weekend, that kids with extra chromosomes weren't institutionalized automatically anymore. How thankful I was that Penny would be able to contribute in a meaningful way to our community. And how much I needed to remember that everyone had more going on—more stress, more pain, more fear—than they ever admitted.

As I lay in bed, I realized that the question I had been asking all day long was, "What can she do?" When I asked it of Penny in comparison to the other kids, she came up short every time. But I finally thought to ask, "Who is she?" and I started to remember all the traits that were unique to her—the slobbery kisses, the eyes that followed me around a room, the laughter and sweetness. And when I asked that question of the other kids, I didn't come up with answers based upon how they might perform on a test, but answers based upon their personalities. I thought about Ellen Grace wanting to hold her dad's hand whenever he was in the room, or the way Simon reached out his arms for his mother, the way Josie carried her blue teddy bear wherever she went. There was no need to compare the answers to "Who are you?" It was just a way to find the good, the particular, about anyone. And it made me realize that our daughter's character measured up to everyone else's. She couldn't walk or run. Ten years from now she might not be able to do multiplication tables at the same rate as the other children her age. She might not be reading the same books. But if I thought about her in terms of her character, and not some set of competencies, then I could embrace her alongside her peers.

We took a photograph of all five kids on the sofa the next morning. The parents swarmed the room with cameras and exaggerated happiness. One by one, each of our children began to cry until all five of them were in the arms of a mother or father. They weren't that different after all.

My favorite things Penny is doing these days include "blow," where she puffs out air and causes her bangs to fly up; "bath," where she rubs her belly with both hands, grinning and twisting side to side; and "Down came the rain and washed the spider out," where she waits, hands above her head, and lets them fall and then shimmies her shoulders and demonstrates "washed out."

Her communication ability surprises me every day. I started to teach her the sign for "car" a few days ago, but hadn't tried again since. This morning I said, "Penny, we're going in the car," and she responded with the sign. Every day she learns more and more.

April 2007

17

In early February, Penny awoke in the middle of the night. She was coughing, and it sounded painful, like a dog barking. Peter and I both hurried into her room. We rubbed her back until she fell asleep again. The next morning, there were traces of that raspy sound, but she was cheerful. I made a doctor's appointment just to be safe.

Dr. Bill was more concerned than I expected. He prescribed an antibiotic, Tylenol, and decongestant around the clock. That afternoon, her head felt feverish. She refused to eat lunch, and the barking cough returned. I rocked her to sleep.

An hour later, Peter stopped into the apartment between classes and his squash practice. He found me at my computer and said, "Age, I was listening to Penny while I changed my clothes. She doesn't sound good."

She was awake, coughing. Her eyes looked glassy.

"Let's take her temperature," I said.

We laid her on her back. She coughed again, but this time she started to choke. The color drained out of her face, from pink to white to blue.

Somehow we found ourselves driving to the emergency room—me clutching Penny to my chest as Peter ran red lights and exceeded the speed limit and passed cars on a double yellow line. Penny was limp and pale and we could barely keep her awake, even with the windows down and cold air pumping. As she slumped over my shoulder, I focused my attention on her hands. I kept saying, "How big is Penny?" in the most cheerful voice I could muster, and I watched for a flicker of movement. She didn't have the strength for her usual response—both arms up with a big smile—but I saw her fingers move every time I said it. Then her eyes would close and her body would go limp again, and I tried to ignore the panicked voice in my head. I told myself, "She's just tired. Her nap was interrupted. She's going to be fine."

Throughout the car ride, I pushed away thoughts that she might not make it. It was as if I had a ticket to cash in with God. *You can't let anything happen to her. Not now. You promised. The Lord protects the simple-hearted.*

What should have been a twelve-minute ride to the emergency room took seven. Holding Penny close, I ran through the sliding doors. "My daughter needs a doctor right now!"

The woman behind the desk looked up. "What's the problem?"

"I don't know. We were changing her diaper and she started coughing and turned blue." I looked at Penny. She still lay against my shoulder, but her eyes were open now, scanning the room.

"Okay. I'll get you to a nurse as soon as possible."

"No," I said. I felt my face harden. "I need to see a doctor right now."

A nurse approached us. "I'll take you in here, honey. It's going to be fine."

I could hear Penny's labored breathing. Her heart pounded through the blanket, but her eyes were open and focused. We sat down. The nurse took Penny's temperature—103—and Penny offered me a wan smile.

"In the car, she couldn't lift her head," I said. "She seems a little better now."

"Sweetie," the nurse said. "I know this is scary. But your daughter is going to be fine. I'm going to take you to a bed right now."

Peter had parked the car, and he walked in just as we headed back to our section of the ER, a small bay with a chair and a stretcher.

After a flurry of initial tests, Penny slept on my chest, naked except for a diaper and a pink blanket pulled over her back. Her hair was matted with sweat, a blood oxygen monitor hugged her big toe, and three cotton balls with tape on them marked the places they had drawn blood. But her body was calm. I could feel the soft whisper of her breath on my neck. Sitting in the dim light, with the beeps and general commotion of the ER outside the curtain, I wasn't thinking about anything. All I wanted was this moment, this peaceful security. I was totally content with nothing to do other than hold my baby girl and feel her sleeping safely in my arms.

Within a few hours, her fever had gone down to 100. Her cheeks were rosy, and she was sitting up in bed, waving to the hospital personnel. Chest X rays revealed bronchitis, and her white blood count was slightly higher than normal, but not high enough to pose grave concern. The doctor assumed she had choked on a large wad of phlegm that had begun to dislodge itself by the time we reached the hospital. They discharged us five hours after we arrived, with instructions to check on her every hour throughout the night.

One of the nurses brought Penny a gift when we were in the hospital—a soft white dog with the words "*Jesus me ama*" written in pink on its bib. Penny beamed whenever we wound it up and listened to the song. And as it played that simple tune, with words that hearkened back to the faith of a child, I could only nod my head.

Yes, Penny. Jesus loves you. As do we. Very, very much.

Penny recovered from her bout with bronchitis, but I started to linger in her room in the evenings just before I went to bed. I watched her asleep in her crib—on her side, one leg crossed over the other, tangled up in her blanket, breathing peacefully. And I wondered whether it would ever be possible for me to love another child the way I loved her, to experience joy and pride and sorrow and fear for anyone else to the same degree I did for her. I looked at her sleeping there and thought, *You are perfect. Perfect.*

And yet every night I was also thinking about a very real imperfection in her body, that little opening between her heart and her lungs. We were due for another hospital visit at the end of February, this one planned months in advance. For weeks, I thought about what was coming. I reviewed the questions I had asked the cardiologist, the assurances I had received that this outpatient procedure would be easy and painless. Penny would check in to the Children's Hospital of Philadelphia for the day. A surgeon would insert a catheter and a camera through her groin in order to repair the hole. If all went well, we would bring her home that night.

Fifty percent of children with Down syndrome were born with heart defects. Oddly enough, I hadn't ever considered Penny to be in that category. To me, "congenital heart defect" implied emergency open-heart surgery. Bandages. Wounds. Long hospital spells. Not an outpatient procedure. Not the doctor's words, "She'll be fine the next day. No pain. No discomfort." Her heart problems were minor compared to some other kids with Down syndrome. I knew parents whose children had been in the hospital for weeks after a much more significant reconstruction. And yet once I realized that Penny's heart was one of the "defective" ones, it helped me understand how little a list of problems in a book could capture the reality of our particular experience, of her particular life.

On the day of the procedure, Penny woke up and used a sign spontaneously for the first time. She looked me in the eye, then raised her hand to her mouth and patted her lips. *Eat*. We had been working on sign language for a few months. Dr. Post had recommended it, and I had been convinced by recent studies that showed that all children could understand the world before they could speak. Penny's ability to form words would be even more delayed than a typical kid's, so we figured signing would help us bridge the gap. We picked five signs with practical application—eat, drink, more, get down, and all done—and we repeated them all day long. At every meal, before Penny ate anything, I showed her the sign for eat. And then I took her hand and moved her fingers to her mouth, all the while saying out loud, "eat." Only after she had mimicked the sign would I give her food. But that morning was the first time she had used a sign without any prompting.

"Oh sweetie, I'm so sorry. You aren't allowed to eat today."

Her big blue eyes didn't waver. *Eat,* she signed.

Peter, who had been outside clearing the car of snow, walked into her room. She turned her head to him and signed, *Eat.*

"I'm sorry, kiddo. Try to remember that one for tomorrow." Peter scooped her into his arms.

I had learned the details of the procedure the week before. Penny had a PDA, a patent ductus arteriosis, an open blood vessel between her lungs and her heart. It put her at risk for pulmonary hypertension as a young adult. The hole existed for every newborn, so Penny's initial echocardiogram hadn't raised any concern. But for most children, the hole closed on its own within the first few days of life. Penny's wasn't getting any smaller. So they would insert a catheter with a camera into her heart to see how much blood was flowing through the hole. Then they would drop a metal coil into place, wait to make sure blood pooled on either side of the coil, indicating that the hole was closed, and release her. We would spend six hours in the recovery room and then go home. And that should be that.

After our ride to the emergency room a few weeks earlier, Peter had told me, "I thought we were going to lose her." But I had refused to worry, even with Penny limp in my arms. It was impossible for me to imagine a world without her.

Penny lay on a table in a purple gown that swallowed her body. Technically, she wasn't even big enough to qualify for the procedure. Fourteen months old. Sixteen pounds. Still wearing clothes designed for babies half her age. She screamed as the nurses took her vital signs, and I wondered how much she remembered about her hospital visit from a few weeks earlier. Peter and I each held one arm, and I kissed the tears that streamed down her cheeks as a technician inserted the IV. But as soon as the poking and prodding was done, Penny sat up. We sang her favorite songs and played until another nurse arrived to give her a sedative and put her to sleep.

Two hours later, they were done. The hole was closed. But we had six hours to go in the recovery unit. I had thought we were waiting to ensure that Penny had recovered from the sedation, but her nurse gave us further instructions. "You need to keep her on her back with her legs straight and still," she said, checking Penny's monitors and giving her a sip of juice.

"Straight and still?"

"Yep. We need to make sure that her wounds don't open up or bleed too much or cause her to lose circulation."

I nodded, wondering if my face betrayed me. *Oh. That's all. Explain to my fourteen-month-old daughter that she should lie still for six hours. Of course.*

Penny was sleepy at first. She gave us a little wave, but no smile. Her eyes were bleary, she had pressure bandages on both legs, five wires connected to her chest, a blood oxygen monitor, a blood pressure cuff, and an IV. Her skin looked pale, her body limp. Then she began to wake up, and she also began to fight. All the color drained from her face and her lips and she vomited. Her tongue hung out of her mouth. But soon she settled down and dozed. She was never fully asleep. The whole time, if Peter or I moved away, her eyes fluttered open and she would struggle until she could feel the assurance of one of our hands upon her own.

We took her home that night. I was relieved to drive away, relieved to know that this little hole that only a few years ago would have required a surgical incision and a week in the hospital, this little hole that decades earlier would have guaranteed early death, this little hole was closed forever. We would return for an echocardiogram in ten days just to be sure. After that, she needed to be monitored every three to five years. But my relief went beyond my concern for Penny. I was also relieved to get away from the bright white linoleum floors and the beeping monitors and the sadness. The room with a message on the window: Happy 13th birthday, Laura.

The next day Penny slept more than usual, and I winced to see the bruise that covered most of one of her thighs, but otherwise she seemed like herself. She repeated her feat of the previous morning and signed, *Eat*. Already, she had more energy. She started to hurl herself backward when sitting up, usually with a quick glance behind to make sure she would land on a soft surface. She stood at the ottoman, needing less support than ever. She started to make sounds I hadn't heard before.

Missy, the therapist who had known her the longest, came for her weekly visit three days after Penny's time in the hospital. They went through their normal routine—moving from sitting to stomach, rolling over, pushing herself back to sitting, pulling herself up to stand. Then Missy looked at me with a smile. "This child is ready to do physical therapy."

"What do you mean?" I frowned, thinking back to the work we'd been doing for the past year.

"That heart procedure made a huge difference. She's so much stronger already."

It made sense. Penny's body had been working inefficiently, and now the blood was flowing where it was supposed to. But it still came as an unexpected gift. I had thought the procedure would simply prevent illness later in life, not give her energy today. It inspired me. When Missy left, I set up an appointment to have Penny fitted for ankle braces, and I contacted a man who made mini treadmills for kids with Down syndrome to help them learn how to walk.

Penny's cognitive abilities seemed different after the surgery, too. She was already on the road to signing, but throughout the month of March her learning accelerated. Within a week she had added *more* and *get down* to her signing vocabulary. And then a few weeks after that, I was trying to get her to move from sitting up to lying on her stomach, so I placed a toy just out of reach on a blanket and went into the kitchen for a glass of water. When I returned, she was still sitting up, and she had the toy. Instead of toppling over to grab it, she had pulled the blanket closer. She had outsmarted me.

I thought back to that visit almost a year earlier with the genetic counselor who told us Penny would never be able to problem-solve. She had given the example of Penny walking to school. She said Penny would be able to memorize the route, but she wouldn't be able to figure out an alternate route if for some reason her regular path were obstructed. But this toy in her lap seemed like pretty good problem solving to me.

It wasn't long before Penny was putting her signs together. *More drink. More book.* And then came the moment. It was mid-April and a nor'easter was pummeling the East Coast. After her nap, I held Penny on my hip and we looked out the window at the storm. "Look, Penny, it's raining," I said, and I demonstrated the sign for rain, my fingers wiggling down through the air.

She looked outside, looked at me again, and mimicked my motion.

Then I pointed to a tree. "Tree," I said and pivoted my arm from elbow to hand. Again, she looked, thought, and mimicked.

And I knew that something had changed. She wasn't learning by rote anymore. Something connected in her brain and helped her understand that every object had a corresponding word. From then on, instead of spending a week working on a single sign, she picked up words every day. Before long, her signing vocabulary went from a dozen to fifty or more. I bought a *Dictionary of American Sign Language* to keep up.

In the midst of Penny's growth spurt, I read a book by Michael Bérubé called *Life As We Know It*. Bérubé was a professor of English, and his book contained his philosophical and practical reflections about Down syndrome in general and about his son Jamie in particular. In one chapter, Bérubé discussed the sociology of Down syndrome. He explained how our "scientific" understanding of trisomy 21 had changed over the course of the twentieth century. For example, parents who had a son or daughter with Down syndrome a century ago were told, in contrast to the average IQ of 100, their child would have an IQ between 20 and 40. Doctors stated that these kids would be "profoundly mentally retarded," would never speak or read, never solve problems, possibly never learn to walk. Down syndrome was a tragedy. By mid-century, parents of children with Down syndrome were told to expect an IQ between 40 and 60, with possibilities for walking and talking, but no chance of independent living and a drastically curtailed life expectancy. Now Penny's life expectancy was double that of a child born with Down syndrome even twenty years earlier. And literature from Dr. Post told us to expect an IQ between 60 and 80. And I had to wonder, *Who knows what doctors will be telling parents of children with Down syndrome in another thirty years?*

When Penny was born, expectations I didn't even know I had rose to the surface and were shattered by the words *mental retardation*. In the early months of her life, I had reset those expectations. I came to peace with the idea, or, as I then believed, the reality, that though Penny's intelligence would be limited, her spirit could soar. I grew accustomed to the thought that Penny wouldn't ever be "book smart," but that her personality and her "emotional intelligence" would be off the charts. And that seemed fine to me, even somewhat exciting and good. But Bérubé's simple progression of IQ predictions suggested I should give up any attempt to predict Penny's limits going forward.

She began to achieve many of her developmental milestones "on time." She showed her knowledge of the purpose of common objects by tapping her socks to her feet.

She demonstrated an understanding of cause and effect by turning on and off light switches. She learned new words. I had to adjust my expectations again. And this time I said, *Who knows? Who knows if my child will join a book club or love poetry? Who knows if she'll sing in a choir or dance in a recital or speak in public? Who knows if she'll drive a car or get married or have children of her own? Who knows if she'll have a best friend or a boyfriend or sibling rivalry?*

I didn't know what she would be able to do, but I hoped for more and more. I understood that this extra chromosome of Penny's would slow her down sometimes. But I was no longer willing to trust the experts who tried to tell me exactly how she would be slowed down, or to what degree. Instead, I was willing to wait and see. I didn't have specific expectations for her athletic endeavors as a teenager or her college degree or her spouse. I simply expected that over and over again, I would be surprised, and delighted, by our daughter.

Every day it becomes more and more clear that Penny is not a "Down's kid." Penny is a child with wonderful and fascinating aspects to her personality. Penny is a child who knows and loves her family, who has a big vocabulary and loves books, who blows kisses to anyone who says hello, who is learning to climb stairs, and, oh, yes, Penny is also a child who has Down syndrome.

May 2007

18

In the late spring my friend Samantha called. "There's a new baby with Down syndrome, and the parents want to get connected. I'm swamped this week—do you think you could call them back?"

"Sure," I said. "Let me grab a pen and paper."

I took their names and number. When I left a message, I found myself trying to tamp down my own enthusiasm. "This is Amy Julia Becker from the Down Syndrome Association. I hear you have a daughter with Down syndrome, and I just wanted to call to welcome you to our community and answer any questions you might have for another parent. My daughter is sixteen months old, and she's a delight." I left our number and hung up the phone. Penny was on the floor nearby, swaying to her reflection in the mirror.

Linda and John and their daughter, Hope, came over for Sunday brunch. Peter greeted them at the door and led them back to the kitchen. I held Penny on my hip. She waved and said, "Ha!" her version of "Hi!"

"Welcome!" I said.

"Here, let me get that." Peter reached out his hand to take Linda's diaper bag. Hope had been asleep in her car seat carrier, but by the time they made it to the kitchen she had opened her eyes. Linda picked her up, cradling Hope's neck with her hand. I remembered Penny's floppiness at the same age, the way her head would lurch back without warning. I hadn't realized how much stronger she was now.

Linda and John sat down at the kitchen table. Her body looked as rigid as the straight-backed chair. I wanted to hug her and say, "No really—it will all be fine. Your daughter will be your pride and joy. Don't worry!" But I knew that the same words to me a year earlier would have sounded impossible.

Hope was five months old with curly black hair from her mother and round cheeks from her dad. For most of our time together, she sat in Linda's lap without making a sound.

Penny sat in her high chair, banging her hands and babbling. "Baba!" she said.

"What, sweetie?"

She signed, *Eat*.

"Penny's been learning sign language," I said to Linda and John. "It's such a gift because we can understand what she needs."

Linda nodded and gave a tight smile. I recalled the feeling when I first met kids with Down syndrome who were a little older than Penny, how I had wanted to run away, how I had resisted the thought that we might need sign language to communicate or that walking would take a long time or that therapists would be a part of our daily life.

John said, "So, how did you find out that Penny had Down syndrome?"

We shared our stories and discovered that they were like us—they didn't learn Hope's diagnosis until after she was born.

"You know," I said, cracking eggs as I talked, "I don't think about Down syndrome all the time anymore. It might seem strange to say that because it is certainly part of our everyday reality, with the therapists and doctor's appointments and all the rest. But it's different than it was a year ago."

Linda nodded, but she looked skeptical.

Penny smeared yogurt on her cheeks.

I said, "Like the other day, the women who help clean our apartment were here, and I walked into the room. They were holding one of the books we have about Down syndrome and pointing to a little boy on the cover. They seemed so embarrassed when I found them. And I realized that I used to feel embarrassed when people saw that Penny had Down syndrome. But now I want them to know that this is what it can look like." I put down the eggs and motioned toward Penny. "This happy little girl with yogurt in her hair who says hi and is learning sign language and loves giving slobbery kisses. This is what it looks like to have Down syndrome."

Linda and John stayed for about an hour. They asked about therapists and insurance plans and doctors. We told them we'd be happy to help in any way we could. But I also knew that Hope was going to be the one to help them. She would grow up and love them and they would find that their love for her was enough to replace the sadness and the fear. And all the things that seemed so overwhelming would become normal.

After we walked them to the door, I turned to Peter. "You know, Samantha was telling me the other day about when she first got connected to the Down syndrome group. It was late spring, so I guess two years ago, and the first thing she was invited to was the picnic. She said she cried all day at work, and she kept telling people, 'But I don't want to be invited to a Down syndrome picnic!' And now she's going to be a member of the board. She said she can't wait for the picnic this year."

Peter nodded. "I never thought this would be my life. But I love it."

He kissed Penny and held both hands to the side of his cheek, the sign for nap. "Time to go night-night?" he asked her. She held out her arms.

Our time with Linda and John highlighted for me how my view of the world, and of Penny, had changed. But often I forgot that the same transformation hadn't occurred in the people around me. The following weekend, we had three couples over for dinner. Someone asked about Penny's recovery from her heart procedure, and I launched into a description of the past two months. "It's pretty incredible," I said. "She's signing a ton and getting stronger and stronger on her feet."

Peter chimed in, "Have you seen her treadmill?" The mini treadmill had arrived, and Peter had made it his mission to get Penny up and walking. We had set up a big mirror so she could see herself, and after a few weeks of getting steadier on her feet, Penny had started to love it. Peter said, "She's up to three miles per hour, and it's the cutest thing—every so often she lets go of the bar with one hand and waves to herself in the mirror."

Everyone smiled as Peter mimicked Penny's gestures—her happy expression and delicate wave.

"What's amazed me," I said, "is how much repairing her heart seems to have increased her cognition." I recited the information I had learned recently about IQ and then added my own thoughts: "Penny's generation of kids with Down syndrome is so different from the past. They have Early Intervention and they live at home, not to mention all the medical breakthroughs. I wouldn't be surprised if Penny or some of her peers with Down syndrome grow up with normal intelligence."

I could almost touch the discomfort. It wafted through the air like the stench from an open garbage can. One friend lowered her eyes. Another stole a glance at her husband. He said, "But isn't it a false construct to talk about normal intelligence?"

And then his wife: "Haven't you talked a lot about wanting to value things other than intelligence?"

"Yes. Of course. But I just think Penny might be capable of a lot more than we were told when she was first born. Like the genetics counselor who told us she wouldn't be able to add 9+6 without counting on her fingers . . ."

One of the men interrupted, "My wife still has trouble adding 9+6 without counting on her fingers!" Everyone laughed.

I felt myself retreating. It reminded me of my freshman year in college, when I announced to my new friends that upon graduation I would be marrying Peter, who was a senior in high school at the time. Back then, I had seen those same looks—the sympathetic glances, the gentle attempts to make sure I didn't have my hopes in the wrong place. Now I could imagine the unspoken comment, "Sorry. Your kid is retarded. It's as simple as that." Or, "Don't worry. We all love her no matter her IQ."

A part of me wanted to face it head-on, to protest that I had come to accept that Penny's intelligence would be different from mine, that IQ wasn't any way to measure a person's worth, that I really didn't care what school she attended or what grades she got. I wanted to protest that I knew the reality of Down syndrome in far greater detail than any of them—her floppy limbs and difficulty producing consonant sounds and the hearing deficit and raspy voice and all the rest. But I also wanted to protest that Penny solved problems. She communicated. She loved books and music and people. I wasn't willing to argue about it, but I also wasn't willing to deny the reality that my "mentally retarded" daughter was smart.

A few weeks later, we were visiting my parents. Penny had gone to bed, and my mother's book club was meeting in her living room. I entered the conversation at the end of the evening, and one of Mom's friends asked about Penny. Mom and I kept interrupting each other to offer more. Mom said, "As a preschool teacher, it is just wonderful to see how much Penny is able to learn."

I added, "She knows her animal sounds and body parts and she has over one hundred signs."

Mom's friend cocked her head and said, looking at me, "How nice. And does Penny know who you are?"

Just a minute earlier, I had felt like a grown-up version of my daughter, who tended to bounce in place from the excitement of being alive. But the energy leaked out of me as soon as she asked her question. I said, "Yes. My daughter knows who I am." I gave a tight-lipped smile and walked away.

Another woman present said, "Do you think about other children? I'm sure it's hard, since your daughter is such a challenge."

I felt the mask slide into place. "We'd love to have other children. Thanks."

A wall of disdain threatened to separate me from anyone who made an ignorant comment. As I walked upstairs, I told myself I wasn't being fair. I wasn't being gracious. I might have said the same things in the past. But their words stung, and I couldn't let them go.

Around the same time, I came across an article in the *New York Times* about a young man, Jason, with Down syndrome. The writer described Jason's mom, Emily Kingsley. She had insisted on keeping her son home, back in 1974. According to the article, he flourished. He started reading when he was four. He made friends. He appeared on *Sesame Street*, where his mom was a writer, and on other television shows through the years. But then, around six or eight, the other kids passed him. For all his promise and potential, at a certain point his brain couldn't get him "there," wherever that hypothetical point might be.

And I went to sleep wondering if my recent amazement at Penny's ability to learn was ill-founded. If I was just setting myself, and her, up for dashed dreams. If I had just climbed back into a shell of valuing the wrong things and measuring human worth by achievement. The article worried me.

But in the morning I started to consider how I might have been duped. The article upset me because I thought I understood what this mother was thinking. But then I noticed a few other things. First, the writer didn't use "person first" language to describe Jason, but rather called him a "Down syndrome child." And the writer commented that the 1970s marked the divide between "the dark years . . . and modern times." I thought, *Really?* It wasn't so clear to me that modern times were an age of enlightenment when it came to people with disabilities. Sure, we didn't institutionalize them anymore, but the vast majority of women with a prenatal diagnosis of Down syndrome chose abortion. *Out of the darkness, indeed.*

I thought about this mother—her son had appeared on TV and had written a book and now lived and worked independently and seemed to be a very nice man—and I realized there was no way he had disappointed her. The writer of the article might think she ought to feel disappointed, but a reporter might look in on us and see a little girl who was eighteen months old but couldn't walk on her own—and might think we felt disappointed. When all we felt was immense pride.

When I looked at Penny, I saw our daughter—with her big eyes, now sea green in the center surrounded by a thick band of dark blue, with her dad's long eyelashes and her heart-shaped lips. I saw our daughter—who rested her head on my chest and gave me a kiss, who worked hard every day, who had so much to offer. And when I laid her in her crib that night, I prayed that I might remember that her value was intrinsic to her, bestowed already by her Creator, not by a writer for the *New York Times* or by a therapist or a doctor or even by me.

I finally came across the terms I had been looking for when I read an article about the No Child Left Behind legislation. In the article, President Bush was quoted as wanting to usurp the "soft bigotry of low expectations." The soft bigotry of low expectations. That was it. I didn't want to have unreasonable goals for Penny's future, but I also didn't want false assumptions based upon the past to constrain her. I thought back to classes I had taken in college. I had been an African-American Studies minor, and it had fascinated me to try to imagine what it was like to be black in America. I remembered writing a personal essay for a class in which I berated myself for not speaking up one night in the dining hall. A boy at the table, an attractive, lacrosse-playing white boy, had been joking about the idea of dating a black woman, and I had sat silent, absorbing the giggles of my peers. My professor had written back to me and said, "Don't beat yourself up. It wouldn't have changed anything. You have to choose your battles."

I hadn't understood. I had pictured myself walking out of the dining hall or making a witty comment or at least sending him a look of scorn. But my professor seemed to think it hardly deserved a second thought. Maybe my confusion arose because I didn't have any real battles to fight. My only experience of racism was external. In this case, I had witnessed a privileged white boy make a joke about black women. On another occasion, I heard a pair of white women talk about how "the blacks" were only suited for jobs in the service industry—nursing, nannying, housekeeping. The comments bothered me, but I hadn't ever been hurt in a personal way by ignorant remarks. Now, unintentional insults or even benign misunderstandings came my way almost every day. In the public eye—when *Time*, as a joke, coined a new phrase, "celebutard," short for "celebrity retard." Or when preschools never returned my phone calls after I mentioned that our daughter had Down syndrome. Or just the general comments about "Down's kids," as if Penny wasn't visible as an individual, only as a part of a separate category of human being. It was then that I started to understand what my teacher had meant. I had to let some of it roll off.

As a Christian, I knew I was supposed to go further. I should forgive the people who offended me. I should even love them. But I couldn't. I chose to ignore the hurtful remarks as much as I could and instead hold on to the stories, the everyday interactions with our daughter. I wanted to tell the woman from Mom's book club about Penny at breakfast one morning, when I said, "If you put that food in your hair, you can't have any toast." She had looked at me for a long moment, rather sternly, as if calculating how seriously she needed to take my words. And then it dawned on her. She took a handful of food out of her mouth and smeared it from forehead to chin, without touching a hair. I gave her the toast.

I wanted the *New York Times* reporter to hear the story of a night when Penny had insisted on going to the potty. Her dad took her in. Recently, she had loved the potty because she got to read a *National Wildlife Federation* magazine with an article about coyotes. Lying in bed, I had to giggle when I heard her, loud and clear: "Ow-oo! Ow-oo!" Our midnight coyote.

I tried to remember that Penny's presence in my life had changed me, but most people didn't have the chance to spend their time with a little girl with Down syndrome. Most people didn't understand her signs. Most people didn't experience the thrill of hearing her make new sounds. I wasn't ready to forgive, but fighting or taking offense wouldn't get me very far. The best thing I could do was shrug my shoulders at the ignorant comments and trust that the story of our family would speak for itself, that Penny would speak for herself, even if those words came through her hands.

Dear Penny,

You are now twenty months old, and I cannot tell you how proud I am of you, and I could never express how much I love you. Just today, you stood by yourself for five seconds—I know you'll be walking soon. And earlier this week, you used your words and your signs to tell me about our family: Mama, Dada, Penny, and George. You went swimming, and you smeared lasagna all over your face and in your hair, and you told me about dogs and flowers and boats, and you used your signs to say I love you.

When you were first born, I was worried. I didn't know much about Down syndrome, and I was afraid. I'm not worried anymore. I am proud of you—our smart, funny, beautiful, delightful daughter. Thank you for being in our lives.

Love,
your Baba
September 2007

19

Back when Penny was five months old, she had been "dedicated" at church as a way to welcome her into the congregation. Dedications happened once a month or so, and every time, Pastor Mike selected a particular Bible verse to give to the child. For Penny, he chose the opening verses of Psalm 1:

> *Blessed is the man who does not walk in the counsel of the wicked*
> *or stand in the way of sinners or sit in the seat of mockers.*
> *But his delight is in the law of the* LORD, *and he meditates on his law day and night.*
> *He is like a tree planted by streams of water, which yields its fruit in season and whose leaf does not wither.*

When Pastor Mike had offered that verse, I smiled. It was an echo of the gift Virginia had sent before Penny was born, a picture of a young girl with a quote from this same psalm. From early on, I had taken those words as a statement of faith. I had been learning to trust that Penny's life would be one that flourished in its season, that God intended for Penny's life to be a fruitful one.

For me, the orchid that had arrived shortly after Penny's birth embodied this Bible passage, this promise. Despite my fledgling green thumb, the orchid bloomed. And bloomed. And bloomed. In fact, it was in continuous bloom for eighteen months. Over time, the orchid had become a symbol of Penny's existence, a visual reminder that she had flourished. She, like the orchid, was extraordinary, inexplicable, a gift. When Penny was eighteen months old, we left for the summer to spend two months at my parents' beach cottage, and the orchid held twenty-five blossoms with another bud on its way.

But in August, I got a call from the person tending the orchid. He hadn't understood my instructions, and all the petals had fallen to the ground. My throat and chest constricted, as if he had called to relate a tragedy. After I hung up the phone, I walked outside to try to talk some sense into myself. I understood that I was mourning the loss of a plant, but I had an emotional connection to it. This was our Penny orchid. This was the orchid that would be in bloom forever, just like our daughter.

We sat outside as a family that evening. The table was set with one of my favorite summer meals—squash casserole and grilled pork, fresh local tomatoes drizzled with balsamic vinegar. My parents and my three sisters filled the seats at the table. The sun was setting over the marsh. It was cool enough to pull a sweater around my shoulders. It should have been an idyllic evening, but I found my mind drifting toward regret. I was afraid that the orchid was a harbinger of things to come.

I tried to join the dinner conversation, but I couldn't find a place to jump in. Kate leaned over at one point and asked, "Are you okay?"

I nodded, aware that the focus of attention had shifted to me. "I know it's silly. I'm just upset about Penny's orchid. I don't know if I'm feeling superstitious or negligent or what. At the very least I feel like a bad mother because I let the stupid plant die."

No one seemed to know what to say about the orchid, but the conversation turned to Penny. First, Elly giggled. "My favorite thing Penny's doing these days is signing *aunt*. She looks like a little prize fighter." Elly mimicked the sign—the letter *A*, a closed fist, shaken near the jawbone.

Mom said, "You all don't even know how much she asks for you when you're away. She takes the phone from the receiver and signs, *Aunt, phone, please,* over and over until I distract her or call one of you."

I felt a smile coming on in spite of myself.

Brooks said, "But the best is when she blows her nose. How does she make so much noise come out of that tiny body? It's hysterical."

I thought about the moment in early June when Penny grasped her nose and looked at me knowingly and made a loud noise. It had taken a few times for me to understand that she was blowing. Loudly. Obtrusively. Just like her dad did when he had a cold. She had learned that the noise got an enthusiastic reaction from her aunts, so it had become a staple of their interactions.

As my sisters talked, the images poured through my consciousness. Penny swimming with her dad. Sitting in her stroller and waving to every passerby as if she had been hired to greet them. Chiming in at the end of a song. And as I thought about Penny—delightful, charming, smart, wonderful Penny—I realized that I didn't need that orchid any longer. For almost two years it had stood as a symbol of my hopes for our daughter. It had even stood as a source of metaphorical protection against all my fears of what might be. But I didn't need a symbol anymore. Penny was flourishing, with or without an orchid to prove it.

We were headed back to Lawrenceville that fall, and I had enrolled Penny in preschool for the first time, two mornings a week. She would also move from the nursery into an official Sunday school classroom at church. I wanted everyone—Penny's teachers, the other students in her classes, and the parents of the other students—to be able to see her for who she was. I sometimes felt as though Penny's life were a document with all sorts of fascinating words written across the page and also with a big red stamp that read, "Down syndrome." I had started to ignore the stamp and read the other words. But I was worried other people wouldn't be able to do the same.

So I got to work. I had Peter handle the camera as he videotaped Penny sitting on my lap, demonstrating dozens of signs. When I went back to watch the recording, I realized that her signs for cat, sleep, phone, and home were virtually indistinguishable. All of them originated on the side of the face. It was rare that I failed to understand her, but to an outsider watching the video, it looked dubious. I tried to remind myself that this was the school that had called me back, that theirs was the director who said, "We've had children with special needs before. I don't think it will pose a problem. It will be good for everyone to have Penny with us."

Peter pushed the stroller as we walked Penny to her first day of school on a sunny morning at the end of August. She wore a dress her Nana had made for her Aunt Kate decades earlier—white fabric with an embroidered bunny rabbit. Her hair had glints of blond from the summer sun, and her eyes sparkled at the sight of five other children surrounded by books, dolls, and toys. The teachers invited us to stay so Penny would feel comfortable in her new setting.

I used the time to assess the other kids. Penny was the oldest in the class by five months, and the smallest by a few inches. There were two other children who weren't yet walking. By that point, Penny had become a proficient scooter, using her heels to propel her body wherever she wanted to end up. As soon as we entered the classroom, she scooted over to the basket filled with dolls and spent a good twenty minutes lining them up on the floor and then putting a blanket over them, hugging and kissing and occasionally mauling them. In the midst of watching the children clamber around the room, one of Penny's teachers said, "It's nice that none of them are talking yet. They're all on the same level."

Only a few minutes earlier, I had explained that Penny used sign language to communicate, and I had handed over my video. I was already feeling self-conscious. I told myself, *You're turning into that mother, that ridiculous, takes-everything-too-seriously, over-involved mother.* But I couldn't resist. I said, "Penny is talking, actually. She's just talking with her hands."

Miss Carol nodded. "Of course."

About half an hour later, Penny scooted close to me. She said, "Baba," and then she signed, *Home.*

Our introduction to the toddler class at church had started months earlier. When we were away over the summer, the director of Children's Ministries had emailed me: "Anne Kass has volunteered to serve as Penny's Buddy in Sunday school this year."

After I received the message, I closed my eyes and took a deep breath. I knew the good intentions. She wanted to ensure that Penny didn't take up a disproportionate amount of the teacher's time, and she wanted to keep Penny safe in the midst of bigger children who might knock her over. But I hated the thought of Penny being singled out presumptively. I hated the image of her in the corner with an adult, while all the other kids played with each other. I worked it out in my mind. If Penny had a Buddy now, she would always have a Buddy. She would always be the kid who needed special attention. She would always be set apart. So I wrote back, "Thanks so much for the offer of a Buddy for Penny. I don't think it's necessary at this point. Perhaps we could see how things go for a few weeks and then reassess."

When I picked Penny up at the end of her first class, the head teacher said, "Penny paid attention just like all the other kids!"

I held back the sarcastic thought that wanted to spill forth. *No way! At home, she just sits in the corner and drools.* Instead, I said, "I'm so glad. I think you'll find that as long as someone can help her in and out of her chair, she's pretty much like the other children."

I tried to remember that none of the teachers had training with kids with special needs. They were volunteering their time. They had no obligation to become familiar with sign language or therapy plans. And they were a part of a routine that only happened once a week. They were doing their best to serve my child.

And then there were the doctors. That fall, I took Penny through the rounds of specialists: the developmental pediatrician, the ENT, the eye doctor. Six months earlier, the ophthalmologist had diagnosed Penny as farsighted. But, she said, there was no need to think about glasses for a few more years. "She'll just make you mad by taking them off all the time." Over the summer, I had been talking to a friend with a typically developing son about the same age as Penny. It turned out that he had the same degree of visual impairment as Penny, and his doctor had insisted on glasses right away. Maybe it was just a difference in physicians, but I couldn't help thinking that when our doctor had seen a kid with Down syndrome, she had decided to try to make my life easier by waiting to prescribe the glasses.

Everywhere we turned, I found people with marvelous intentions and misplaced compassion. As the heat of summer waned and the leaves began to show streaks of yellow and red, I found myself longing for the protection of the summer, the safe place of my family's cottage, far away from schools and churches and doctors and all those people who didn't understand.

Even with close friends it could be difficult. Virginia came to visit in October, along with her three-month-old daughter, Kristin. On the night they arrived, Penny was ready for a bath, so after a quick hello, Virginia joined me in the bathroom. Penny sat in the tub, splashing merrily, and Virginia interrupted her own sentence to say, "Hey, actually, can I throw Kristin in there, too?"

"Sure," I said. "Go for it."

"I mean, Penny won't freak out or anything, will she?"

"I don't think so." I looked at Penny with her perennial smile. "Penny, sweetie," I said, "when baby Kristin gets in the bath with you, you need to be very gentle."

Penny stopped splashing as soon as Kristin lay next to her and she signed *baby, bath*. It didn't take long to finish the bath and get them ready for bed, and within an hour both were fast asleep. Virginia and I retreated to the living room.

"Amy Julia," Virginia said. Her tone of voice alerted me that a serious comment was on its way. She held my gaze for a minute before she looked down at our plate of cheese and crackers. "Sometimes I feel so self-conscious when I talk to you about Penny. I'm afraid I'll say the wrong thing, and I'll hurt you. I get so awkward." She sat back and took a sip of wine. "I mean, like in the bath tonight. I didn't mean to say that thing about Penny freaking out. I wouldn't have said it if she didn't have Down syndrome. I just felt stuck—like what if I'm being insensitive for not asking, but what if I'm making a false judgment if I do ask. . . . I guess I'm just hoping you'll believe me when I say I'm trying."

I opened my mouth, but then I closed it again. I hadn't realized that the bath comment was unusual. Virginia had three kids, so I figured she was just thinking of Penny as an only child who hadn't bathed with a baby before. I was about to dismiss her comment altogether, but I thought back to other things she had said in the past. Like the time she had told me Penny was my "cross to bear." The thought had struck me as somewhat absurd—the image of lugging Penny around like a burden of grief or guilt or punishment. Or the time she had said it was a relief Penny wouldn't know that she was different when she got older. I had wanted to snap at her then. *What, she won't be smart enough to know people are making fun of her? She'll be too much of a sweet Down's kid to feel sad?* But even at the time, I knew she was trying to understand, and so I had disagreed as gently as I knew how. I still remembered the comments, but they hadn't gotten in the way of our friendship.

Virginia said, "See, here I go again. I'm trying to figure out what's going on with you right now, and I can't read your face."

I smiled and pulled my legs under my body. "Start with not being so worried. Really. We're fine. I actually had no idea that you were being weird about the bath earlier, for better or for worse. I'm just trying to think of how to respond." I tapped my finger against my lip. "Okay, the thing is, you have said things that have hurt me in the past. But what I love about you and about our friendship is your candor. I love it that you speak your mind and that I don't have to second-guess what you're thinking. I love it that you don't hold back. A lot of what you have to say is exactly what I need to hear. I'd rather have the hurtful stuff, or the awkward stuff, or whatever, and trust that it will work out in the end."

I munched on a cracker for a minute and then said, "I read a book recently that distinguished between pity and compassion. The author said that they can seem very similar, but pity is when someone looks at your life and says, 'I'm so sorry.' And the way they say it involves a distancing mechanism, as if they're holding up a hand to stop you from getting any closer. And what they really mean to say is, 'I'm so glad that's not my life.' I feel the pity people have for us. Like when someone comes up to me at church and says, as if my mother just died, 'I'm praying for you all,' and pats me on the arm. I can tell that they aren't with me. They just feel bad for us.

"The difference is that compassion also says, 'I'm so sorry,' but it says it as a way of moving closer, of sharing the burden, of coming into the life of the person in need." I thought about a man at church who said hello to Penny with a big grin every week and how when he said, "I'm praying for you," I received his words as if they were a hearty meal on a cold day. Virginia's presence was like his. Safe and loving. I said, "And even though you haven't always said the right thing, I know that everything you've said has been out of compassion. It has always been trying to get closer, trying to understand, trying to be in this with me. I get that. And I'm really grateful for it."

Her face softened. "Bear with me, okay?"

The next day we were sitting on the floor in the playroom. Once Kristin was down for her nap, Penny scooted next to Virginia. She signed, *Read, please,* and they sat together for the next twenty minutes, paging through book after book. I felt relieved that they could interact so naturally, and yet I also found myself about to jump in. It was as if I wanted Penny to perform—to prove all the things she could do, the new signs and colors and sounds. But I kept my mouth shut as Penny climbed into Virginia's lap and listened to my friend read her a story.

We all took a walk later that day. Penny, as always, sat forward in her stroller, poised to greet anyone we passed. Kristin batted at the toys above her head.

"Tell me how your kids are doing," I said. Virginia had two older children—her daughter was five, and her son was almost three, a year older than Penny.

"They're great. Being with Penny makes me miss James, actually. I wouldn't have said it at first. He's really physical. He's been walking forever, and he's huge compared to her. But he's really social, just like she is. Actually, Penny has a bigger vocabulary than he did a year ago, and she certainly likes books more than he does. Sarah's doing well, too. She's five going on thirteen, so we're wondering if it would be good for her to be in an all-girls school."

Penny looked up at me and pointed. She made the sign for squirrel.

"That's right, sweetie. I see the squirrel."

"Amy Julia," Virginia said. "I know you don't like this word, but I'm going to say it anyway. Your daughter is not retarded."

Once again, I didn't know what to say. I finally responded, "I used to think the words *mental retardation* meant that everything in Penny's life would be slower. But now I just think that I have a child with some physical delays who will probably have some learning disabilities, but we don't know what those are."

We returned to the apartment an hour later, cheeks rosy, our noses cold to the touch. I carried Penny up the stairs to our apartment and she scooted into the living room. I followed after her, and something on the windowsill caught my eye. It was the orchid. A shoot had begun a few weeks earlier, and now a bud had appeared. I shook my head. There was more growth to come.

Penny was given a Madame Alexander doll and stroller today. Little did the giver know how appropriate a gift it was, but as Penny is happy to tell the world: "There is a baby in Mommy's belly!" (She does this through signing, with the sign for baby, pointing to my belly, and then saying "Baba," her name for me.) We're expecting Becker #2 around August 12, and, from what we can tell, Penny is very excited to be a big sister.

February 2008

20

At the end of October, Penny had taken three independent steps. She was just shy of twenty-two months old. We cheered and called family members and announced the achievement to everyone we knew. Penny started to pull herself up and immediately let go of the support just to revel in the independence of standing on her own two feet. It only compounded our delight to see the big smile across her face.

Those steps brought me back to the first meeting we had attended with the other parents of young children with Down syndrome, and I remembered the pit in my stomach when I heard about the eighteen-month-old who wasn't crawling or walking. Back then, I had vowed that Penny would be different, as if somehow it was a mark of shame to have a child who didn't walk at the time most pediatricians would predict. But I had grown accustomed to the idea that Penny wouldn't walk until she was at least two. More than that, I had learned *why* she wasn't walking. I could see how hard it was for her to control her limbs and coordinate their movements. It was as if every gross motor skill consisted of ten components. Most kids went through numbers one through ten all at once, with a little trial and error. For Penny and other children like her, each component took work. So those three halting steps, in my mind, were an even greater accomplishment than they would have been a year earlier with a different child.

That fall, Penny and I spent much of our time in the playroom with a space heater nearby. The sunlight had begun to wane in the afternoon, and the cool air rushed through the grand old windows in our apartment. Three days a week, a different therapist joined us for an hour of instruction. Missy continued to work on Penny's gross motor development—walking and learning to use her core muscles. Sharon used "purposeful play" to challenge Penny's cognitive skills. They matched shapes and built blocks and read books. Carolyn worked on Penny's speech.

I could only assume their presence was making a difference. In November, Penny said "Mamama" for the first time, and she managed a "moo" (up until then, cows said "mmm"). She picked up a baby one day and said "wawa," and entertained her dad when he walked in the door with her impression of a gorilla, "hoo hoo," and corresponding arm motions.

Penny was becoming her own person, enjoying the world in her own way, whether by counting pieces of toast, sitting on the floor of her room and "reading" books, pleading for one more round of Tickle Me Elmo, or doing the motions for "Head, Shoulders, Knees, and Toes." She started saying "yeah," with the inflection of a teenager, and "wow" as often as possible. I no longer felt that old ache of fear and worry and guilt underneath the love and pride and joy. It was fun just to be with her.

As Penny approached her second birthday, I discovered I was pregnant. That, too, felt different from the year before. The line on the test was an unambiguous blue. I felt confident from the start that this baby would make it. I didn't tell anyone, though, other than Peter. We celebrated Christmas and Penny's birthday and I hugged my midsection and thought about the bundle of cells inside, cells that already had multiplied enough to form a heart and a teeny body, cells that were becoming our son or daughter.

In early January I had my first prenatal appointment with Dr. Mayer. "Congratulations!" she said. "Let's go ahead and get an ultrasound scheduled so you can see the heartbeat."

I smiled at the thought.

"And we need to talk about prenatal testing." Her words, as upbeat and matter-of-fact as they were, nonetheless made me feel uncomfortable.

"I don't need to know if the baby has Down syndrome," I said. "But I do think we should try to find out if there are heart defects or other physical abnormalities."

She nodded and leaned back against the wall. "Have you and Peter talked about this? Sometimes, you know, it's different for each member of a couple."

I liked Dr. Mayer, but I hated having to defend our choices. I knew she was trying to help, trying to make sure that I didn't do something I would regret, but I wanted her to trust my marriage, to trust our love for Penny, to trust our faith that every human life was a gift, no matter how it arrived. I closed my eyes for a moment. "I'm sure he agrees with me," I said.

"Okay. Then let's have an ultrascreen at eleven or twelve weeks," she said.

"I'm not sure that's necessary," I replied. I had heard about ultrascreens from a doctor friend. They were a new kind of test that identified Down syndrome early on in pregnancy. To me, they seemed like a way to arrange for an early abortion if the markers were positive.

She pushed back. "It's a test that looks for Down's, yes, but it also takes a detailed look at the heart. It's just a way of getting more information."

I swallowed hard. "Okay." I was unable to shake my sense that a cloud had passed in front of the sun.

The shadow persisted throughout the pregnancy. Despite the excitement of it all, I felt as if I had to don a protective vest before entering the world of medical and cultural assumptions about what type of baby I would want, about who would be acceptable to me.

I wasn't worried about the baby having Down syndrome in a general sense, but I was worried about having a baby with major physical complications. I went into the ultrascreen appointment fearful of heart defects, and I lay on the table with cold blue gel across my abdomen, trying to keep my breathing calm and even.

The technician showed me the baby's beating heart and talked me through it as she measured the baby's body parts and drew my blood. "I'll be back with the doctor in a few minutes," she said.

When he arrived, I was certain he was about to deliver bad news. But he said, "This baby's heart looks fine," and my whole body relaxed. "There are no markers for Down syndrome that I can see, but that's better determined through the blood test."

Later that day, we told Penny that I was going to have a baby. She clapped her hands and touched my belly, and I wondered, *Why wouldn't I want another child just like her?*

A week later, a nurse called to give me the full results of the ultrascreen. "You have a one in ten thousand chance of having a baby with Down syndrome," she said.

"Oh," I replied. My first reaction was one of disbelief, almost of protest. I wanted to say, "But I don't know how to raise a child without Down syndrome." Instead I said, "Thank you." I hung up the phone with a strange sense of disorientation, as if for a moment I didn't know where I was standing. *In the kitchen*, I told myself. *You are standing in your kitchen and this baby does not have Down syndrome.*

The pregnancy continued without incident. I soon unearthed my maternity clothes and pulled out the prenatal yoga video. In mid-March, Peter joined me for a Level Two Ultrasound. Through another series of conversations with Dr. Mayer, I had refused an amniocentesis, but I agreed to the more intensive ultrasound as yet another way to identify any potential physical abnormalities. Throughout the exam, the technician reported on each body part as she scanned it. "Perfect," she said, again and again.

The genetic counselor was less certain. "You do know that these tests are only 85 percent conclusive in identifying Down syndrome?"

"Yes," I said. "We understand. We don't think any further tests are necessary."

Peter squeezed my hand, and I could only imagine we were sharing a memory of the day, almost three years earlier, when we had thought a Level Two Ultrasound was foolproof. Peter said, "We're grateful for the baby, no matter what."

Just as we had with Penny, we asked the technician to write the baby's gender on a piece of paper. Peter and I sat on a bench in the hallway together, side by side, and opened the envelope. "It's a boy!"

"It can't be a boy!" I said.

Peter laughed. "Why not?"

"I don't know what to do with a boy!" I smiled as I said it, but I also felt a growing sense of disbelief. Somehow, as the oldest of four girls, I didn't think it would be possible to raise a boy. "I mean, diaper changes and potty training and activities and everything else . . ."

"It will be great," Peter said. "He will be great. You will be a wonderful mother."

I leaned against his chest with a smile, hands laced across my middle. "I hope so," I said. "At least I know he will have a fabulous big sister."

The next morning I dropped Penny off at school. It was raining, so I kept my head down as I hurried back to the car. A colleague of Peter's, a biology teacher, called across the parking lot, "I didn't know you were expecting!"

I grinned and patted my round belly, "Hard to miss. I'm at the halfway mark."

I opened the car door and wiped water from my face. But she walked toward me and continued, "I assume you've done all the screening on this one to find out, if, you know . . ."

"Well, we found out that we're having a boy," I said. "But I'm not having an amnio."

"But then how will you know if this one has Down's? I mean, when I was having kids, I was already in my late thirties, so I had to have the amnios. It wasn't even a choice."

I could feel the water trickling down the side of my face. "You know, we're really happy with who Penny is, so we're just not that worried about having another child with Down syndrome. It isn't necessary information for us."

"But Penny has a really mild case," she said.

I pulled the hood of my jacket back a bit so I could look her in the eye. "Penny has an extra chromosome in every cell of her body. And she's walking and talking and doing really well."

She stared right back at me. "But aren't you at risk for having another?"

"I know exactly what the risks are." I felt as though I was in a contest between two kids, waiting to see who would blink first. "I've got to get out of the rain," I said.

As I drove home, I told myself she just didn't understand. She didn't mean to suggest that Peter and I wished our daughter didn't exist. And yet that implication rose to the surface every time I was asked about the tests we were doing for the baby in my womb.

I wanted to go back to the parking lot and shake her. I wanted to force her to spend a day with Penny, to watch as Penny told me what she did at school, and the names of her friends, and what she would like for her afternoon snack. I wanted to list all the ways Penny was like other two-year-olds, eating with a spoon and fork, albeit messily, learning her shapes, giving lots of hugs. And I wanted to tell her that asking whether I was at risk for having another child with Down syndrome was akin to asking whether I was at risk for having another child with brown hair, with gorgeous green eyes, with Peter's hand-eye coordination or my love for books. It implied that Down syndrome was something separate from Penny, something that could be extracted, if only we had the proper tools and procedures. But that extra chromosome was intrinsic to Penny's being. To take away Down syndrome would be to take away my daughter.

The same sentiments had come up before. "Aren't you brave to have another child!" from one acquaintance. "Lightning never strikes twice!" from another. And, "Of course, you've done all the testing this time," as if we had been naïve consumers the first go-round, and now we were seasoned professionals. But we didn't have buyers' remorse. And Penny wasn't a product, an object of consumption. She was a human being, with her own particular challenges and her own particular gifts.

I turned on NPR as I drove home, and the story was about a new ethics recommendation from the American College of Obstetricians and Gynecologists (ACOG). It stated that doctors unwilling to provide abortions had an obligation to refer their patients to another physician who would provide the procedure. In the words of the spokesperson on NPR, "If a physician has a personal belief that deviates from evidence-based standards of care . . . they have a duty to refer patients in a timely fashion if they do not feel comfortable providing a given service." I thought about all the women who were offered prenatal tests to screen for Down syndrome. And I had to wonder how much those tests really offered care for those women, for those babies. I knew that new medical guidelines—evidence-based standards of care—suggested that all pregnant women, regardless of age, be screened for trisomy 21. And I knew that studies showed that women who received a prenatal diagnosis of trisomy 21 terminated their pregnancies the vast majority of the time. Evidence-based standards of care resulted, more often than not, in the elimination of people like Penny from our society.

I felt the anger surge. The report came across as so factual, so neutral. But I knew from talking to my friends who had children with Down syndrome that the information about that extra chromosome was rarely delivered in a neutral manner. I thought back to Samantha and the phone call she had received when she was eleven weeks pregnant. "We can schedule the procedure for tomorrow so that the termination happens within the first trimester." Or Catherine, whose amniocentesis had shown trisomy 21, but had also shown the absence of the first chromosome. "Your baby's chromosomal makeup is incompatible with life," she was told. And now I knew Elizabeth and Margaret—both three years old. Running. Signing. Making faces in the mirror. Giggling.

It struck me that I hadn't done my own research about the ultrascreen. When I got home, I looked it up online. As a test, it was 90 percent effective in identifying Down syndrome. It was 50 percent effective in identifying heart defects. I shook my head. My relief had been false. The ultrascreen was a way to make Dr. Mayer feel more confident about the baby's chromosomes. It hadn't been what I wanted at all.

My mind wandered back to the NPR report. ACOG had pitted "personal beliefs" against evidence, as if a physician who was unwilling to perform an abortion had defied the evidence about how to care for this woman, this child. I knew abortion was complicated. I had friends who had terminated pregnancies when faced with the news of fatal heart defects and anencephaly. Their grief was real. Their decisions were made in an attempt to care for their whole families. And yet I had to believe that many women who chose to terminate a pregnancy with a prenatal diagnosis of Down syndrome did so based upon probabilities, fear, and misinformation.

I thought back to the list of potential problems we had received in the hospital after Penny was born. Apparently, "evidence-based standards of care" didn't include the fact that the life expectancy of people with Down syndrome had doubled in the past twenty-five years, or that the average IQ of a person with Down syndrome had doubled over the course of the twentieth century, or that many physical "defects" could be corrected relatively easily due to recent medical advances.

"Evidence-based standards of care" included all the physical problems Penny could face, but not the joy she could bring or the abilities she might have. It didn't include the stories I learned many months after she was born, stories about kids and adults with Down syndrome who played on varsity teams in high school, competed and won national art competitions, swam across Lake Tahoe. Or the simpler stories of kindness and love, of people with Down syndrome just being one more member of one more family. "Evidence-based standards of care" didn't include the reality that all of life is fragile and uncertain, with potential for heartbreak and potential for great delight.

A few weeks later Penny was home sick from school, so I took her with me to my twenty-five-week prenatal visit. The receptionist, the nurses, the doctors always asked about Penny. I had shown them pictures and told them stories, but I hadn't ever brought her with me. I was worried she might not be herself. What if she got shy and wouldn't answer questions? What if memories of other doctors' visits made her cry? But that day she couldn't go to school, and I couldn't reschedule, so we walked together into the waiting room.

Penny climbed onto the chair next to me. With a half dozen expectant mothers watching, Penny said, "Read." We paged through a few books, and she then climbed down and started walking around the room.

Someone asked, "What's your name?"

"Penny," she said, without missing a beat, pointing to her chest.

In the next chair over, another woman said, "How old are you?"

She put up one finger and said, "Two."

"Is your mommy having a baby?"

"Yeah," she said, "boy."

A nurse opened the door. "Becker?"

Penny waved good-bye to her admirers and joined me in the back.

Her presence didn't change the pamphlet on the wall that listed trisomy 21 as an abnormality. But I had to imagine she might have changed one of those women's impressions of what it was like to live with Down syndrome. I had to imagine they had a glimpse of our joy.

We're starting to settle in to life as a family of four, I think. (Although I will confess that Peter and I looked at each other a few nights ago and said, "We're capable adults. How on earth can this be so difficult?") William is eating and sleeping pretty well. Penny is delighted to be a big sister. She offers him food, loves hugging and kissing him, holding him on her lap.

On our first night home, Peter and I put Penny to bed. She folded her hands together and said, "Pray."

"Who do you want to pray for?" we asked.

She nodded. "Wuwum."

And so we prayed for William, and gave thanks to God for both our children.

August 2008

21

One day I found Penny in our front hallway. She was sitting cross-legged with my black pocket Bible in her lap, flipping through the pages.

"Do you know what this book is?" I asked her.

She shook her head.

"It's a book about God and Jesus," I said.

"Oh," she replied, wide-eyed.

"Sweetie, we have a Bible just for you in your room. Would you like to see it?"

Together we padded down the hallway, hand in hand. I took a picture book with stories about Jesus from her shelf. We looped her glasses over her ears and she nestled into my lap. I could feel the baby kicking. We started with the story of Zacchaeus, the little man who wanted to see Jesus.

"See Jesus!" Penny agreed, bouncing up and down. She pointed to the Jesus figure in the story, and I realized that the book never showed His face. All afternoon she repeated, "See Jesus!" until I finally found an image of a man with a flowing robe and shaggy beard. "Jesus probably kind of looked like this," I said.

That night, "Read . . . read . . . Bible," Penny requested. This time we read the story of the little children and Jesus. The disciples tried to turn the children away, but Jesus rebuked them and summoned the children to himself in order to bless them.

At the end I said, "Jesus loves Penny."

She beamed.

"And sweetie, you can talk to Jesus, just like the children in the story."

She nodded, put her hands together, and said, "Pway."

We started reading the Jesus stories daily. She often sat in her room and flipped through the pages on her own. She began reminding me to "pway" before meals and at bedtime. I wasn't sure where the interest came from. Maybe there was more going on in Sunday school than I knew. I was pretty sure her spiritual acuity didn't come from Peter or me. We didn't have family devotions. We didn't listen to Christian radio. Until Penny initiated, I hadn't even been trying to tell her about Jesus. She just seemed to like Him all on her own.

One night at dinner I said to Peter, "How will I ever love another child as much as I love Penny? This is not a rhetorical question. I can't imagine feeling about anyone else the way I feel about her." I rested my hands on the top of my belly, wondering how much the little boy within was going to take me away from the little girl sleeping down the hall.

"I don't think that's how love works," Peter said. "It's not as if you have a set amount of love for Penny and now you have to slice it in half and give some of it to the baby instead. The nature of love is to expand." He reached across the table and placed his hand on mine. "I've had less time with you since Penny was born, and it was a rough transition at first. But it wasn't because I lost your love. It was because your love was expanding to include this other person. And so I went from just knowing you as a wife to knowing you as a mother. Penny is going to go from being a daughter to also being a sister. You'll have more love for her than you ever had before. And you'll love her little brother just as much. I'm sure of it."

As my pregnancy progressed, Peter's words grew within me. I would love this baby, this kicking, wriggling, growing baby boy, just as much as his sister. I might even love them both more than I loved Penny now, hard as it was to imagine.

Once again, at the end of the school year, we headed north to my parents' house in Connecticut. I was moving slowly by then, with eight more weeks until I was due. The days at the shore took on a nostalgic quality. I couldn't lift Penny easily. She no longer fit in my lap. I spent more time than usual watching her interact with the rest of the family. She sat for hours in a plastic wading pool, pouring cups of water and watching the droplets trickle down her arms. Occasionally she emerged to lie next to one of her sunbathing aunts. I would find her outside, on her back, hands behind her head, eyes closed, legs crossed. A little goddess. Every so often, she looked up at me and said, "Happy!"

She started singing songs about the people closest to her: "Nana, Nana, Nanananana . . . Baby, Bay Bay Baby! . . . Dadadada Dada." She tottered close to me and kissed my belly and declared, "Didah!" her word for "sister." In the mornings she would wake up and read books on her own, glasses perched on the end of her nose, as if she were a stern librarian. She was growing up. I started to envision her not just as my little girl, but as our son's big sister.

One night in early August, I came back from dinner at my grandparents' house down the road. It took one contraction for me to know it was time. The pain was deep and prolonged. It took my breath away. Five minutes later, it came again. "We need to call the hospital now," I said. Peter packed our bags while I gave Mom instructions for Penny.

The contractions continued apace, forcing me to brace myself, hands pressed against a wall every five minutes. Labor with Penny had been slow and, for many hours, easy. This was different. I knew the pain would only increase, and I had a sense that this baby would come soon. But before we headed to the hospital, I stood in the doorway of Penny's bedroom. There were tears in my eyes—anticipation of the good things to come, but also the sadness of seeing this chapter of our life close. I stood at the side of her crib, watching her body move up and down in a gentle rhythm. I loved the idea of our family expanding. I loved Peter's point that love would only grow. And yet I would miss the singularity of my relationship with Penny. Bringing another baby into this world was a part of letting her go. Another contraction came. I clutched the bar of the crib, and when the pain passed, I placed my hand on her forehead and then tiptoed out of the room.

Every contraction gripped my midsection as if to strangle the baby out of my body. I tried to breathe deeply, tried to remember to pray. "Pull over," I said just before we entered the highway. I stumbled out of the car, placed my hands on my knees, and vomited.

We entered the emergency room of Yale New Haven hospital around midnight. "I want an epidural," I panted. It took two hours. Peter coached me through the pain the best he could.

"I hate it hate it hate it," I moaned. The contractions were back to back, lasting for two minutes with one minute in between.

The midwife looked at the monitor and said, "This is one dramatic baby."

The epidural numbed the pain enough to doze for an hour. And then, in the very early morning, it was time to push. I remembered Dr. Mayer exhorting me with Penny, but this was a new midwife and a new doctor, and once again I couldn't seem to figure it out. After two hours, the obstetrician decided it was time to intervene. "We'll have to use the vacuum," he said. "These contractions aren't good for either of you."

And a few moments later, there he was, our son, crying a hearty cry. I raised my head from the pillow just to look at him. "Ten out of ten on his Apgar," the nurse said.

I was too weak to hold him on my own, and soon my body began to shake. It took another few hours before I could sit up, but finally I held him in my arms. "Hello, William," I said. "It is very nice to meet you." His face looked puffy, just like Penny's had after she was born. His eyes flickered open long enough for me to see that they were slate gray. He didn't have as much hair as his sister had at birth, but it was dark like hers had been. I stroked the side of his cheek as he nuzzled against my shoulder.

By then, Peter had called our parents and siblings and friends. It was a gorgeous day with wisps of white in the sky and sunshine filling the room. We had a view of the water in the distance. After William returned to the nursery, I called Mom. "How's Penny?" I asked.

"She's taking a nap right now," Mom said. "It was the cutest thing. I told her this morning that her baby brother had been born, but I didn't say anything else. She said, 'Wuwum!' How did she know his name?"

I shook my head, even though Mom couldn't see me. "We've had his name for a few months now, and we only told Penny. But she wouldn't even try to say it out loud. I thought maybe she didn't understand. I can't wait to hear her say it."

"Before she went to sleep this afternoon, she said, 'Mama, Dada, Wuwum.' She definitely understands. I could hear her on the monitor even after I left the room, just repeating your names. I think we'll come visit tomorrow morning, if that's okay."

I didn't want to wait that long, but I knew it made sense. The hospital was thirty minutes away, and I still needed some time to recover from the night before. "Tell Penny we miss her," I said.

When I hung up the phone, Peter was holding William, standing by the picture window that gave us a view of the city. He was named for Mom's father, my grandfather. A few weeks after we found out he was a boy, we had compiled a list of family names, and at first I had wanted one that would be unusual. But as we talked, I realized that what mattered most to me in a name was the character of the person it came from. It mattered to me that we had named Penny for her grandmother. Already I saw signs of Grand Penny—precocious, sharp, caring, beautiful—within our daughter. Similarly, I wanted our son's name to come from someone I admired. Someone I would love for him to be like when he grew up.

And so we named him for my grandfather, a man with a gentle spirit and a quiet faith. A man who laughed out loud on a regular basis and who said, "Hello, beautiful!" or "Hello, my friend!" whenever he saw me. A man who played the harmonica to his great-granddaughter.

William started to fuss, and his noises shook me out of my reverie. I took him in my arms to nurse. It struck me then that there were no tears to shed, no difficult phone calls to make. I felt love for William, but it was mellow and easy, distinct from the ferocious and complicated love I had experienced upon Penny's arrival. My body hurt, but that was it. The pain was contained. It would soon heal. William closed his eyes, and I could feel his breath on the bare skin of my chest.

"He has the same hairline as you do," I said to Peter. And then I laid my head back on the pillow and fell asleep.

As promised, Mom brought Penny to visit the next morning. William was nestled into my shoulder, his legs tucked under his body, as if he missed the tight space of my womb. Penny and Mom stood in the doorway. Penny wore a pink dress with a white cardigan and Teva sandals on her feet.

Peter walked over and squatted down to greet her. "Hi, love," he said. Her eyes were big, taking in the room's equipment and machines.

She stared at the blood pressure cuff. "Squeeze?" she asked, squeezing her own arm.

Peter shook his head. "No, sweetie. No squeeze. You're just here to visit Mama and meet your little brother. But can I have a hug first?"

She held out her arms and they embraced. Then he picked her up and carried her to the bed. William stayed asleep as Peter placed Penny next to me with the bed rail behind her.

"Let's take off those shoes," he said, and together they pulled the straps loose.

"Hi, Penny," I said.

"Mama," she replied, and she blew me a kiss with a dramatic "mmm—aaa."

"Will you give your brother a kiss?"

She blew another kiss in his direction.

"What is his name?" I asked.

"Wuwum!" she said, and then she placed both hands on one cheek, the sign for sleep.

"That's right, sweetie. William is asleep. He sleeps a lot."

She signed *sleep* again, and pointed to herself.

"Oh," I said. "You want to go to sleep?"

She laid her head on my chest, looking at her brother, and giggled. I stroked her hair.

Soon she was sitting up again, and she pulled her foot to her face.

Peter laughed. "Penny, what are you doing?"

She was scratching her nose with her big toe. We often marveled at how flexible she was—one of the perks of low muscle tone.

"Penny," Peter said, "I can honestly say that you can do lots of things that your brother will never be able to do."

She didn't acknowledge him, but instead reached over and pulled William's hair. "Ow," she said. He slept on.

"Show me gentle," I said, and she patted his head with her pudgy fingers. From there, she examined him. "Leg. Arm. Belly. Nose. Eye." With each word, she pointed to the body part, concluding with a good poke in the eye and a squawk from her little brother.

Her eyes got wide.

"It's okay, sweetheart. We just have to remember to be gentle." I took her hand in mine. "Penny, when you were born, you were even littler than William. Can you believe that? But now you are big. You're his big . . ."

She completed my sentence: "Didah!"

"Yes. His big sister. I'm so glad you're his big sister. He's going to love you so much." She leaned against my chest one more time, and then she said, "Bye-bye. Mama. Dada. Wuwum."

I looked up at Mom. "Well then, I guess it's time to go."

Mom lifted Penny off the bed and helped her put on her shoes. They held hands and Penny waved before she walked out the door.

A few minutes later, a nurse took William away so I could sleep. "It feels like a vacation," I said to Peter. We had a lovely view. We had all the help we needed caring for our children. I pictured Penny again, walking out the door, hand in hand with her Nana. I imagined her in the hallway, waving goodbye to anyone in her path, straining to push the elevator button, tiring of walking before too long and reaching her arms up toward Mom. And then I thought back to our time together, all four of us as a family. The only emotion I felt was gratitude.

It was gratitude for William, for his safe arrival and his big gray eyes and his slender fingers and soft skin. Gratitude for his big sister and her kisses and cuddles and bright-eyed smile. But it was more than that. It was gratitude that our previous experience in the hospital really was gone forever. The grief we had felt back then had been transformed. It had turned to joy.

Penny wasn't a perfect child. Neither was William. We weren't a perfect family, and we never would be, at least not by the standards I would have set out for us years earlier. But we were coming closer to our *telos*, our true perfection, because we were learning what it meant to be human, what it meant to be whole.

Amy Julia Becker writes and speaks about family, faith, disability, and culture. A graduate of Princeton University and Princeton Theological Seminary, she is also the author of *Penelope Ayers: A Memoir*. Her essays have appeared in the *New York Times, First Things*, the *Philadelphia Inquirer*, the *Hartford Courant*, the *Christian Century*, *Christianity Today*, and *Books and Culture*. She is a regular contributor to *Her.meneutics*, the *Christianity Today* women's blog. She also keeps her own blog, Thin Places, at www.patheos.com /community/thinplaces/. Amy Julia lives in New Jersey with her husband and her three children. For discussion questions and to read more, go to www.amyjuliabecker.com.

Twenty percent of the proceeds from this book will be given to organizations that care for and share life with people with disabilities, including the Special Hope Network (www.special hopenetwork.com) and L'Arche (www.larcheusa.com).